STANLEY and LIVINGSTONE
and the Exploration of Africa
in World History

Titles *in World History*

**Commodore Perry
Opens Japan to Trade
in World History**
0-7660-1462-2

**Philip II and Alexander
the Great Unify Greece
in World History**
0-7660-1399-5

**Leonardo da Vinci and
the Renaissance
in World History**
0-7660-1401-0

**Pizarro and the
Conquest of the Incan
Empire in World History**
0-7660-1396-0

**Mahatma Gandhi and
India's Independence
in World History**
0-7660-1398-7

**Robespierre and the
French Revolution
in World History**
0-7660-1397-9

**Stanley and Livingstone
and the Exploration of
Africa in World History**
0-7660-1400-2

STANLEY and LIVINGSTONE
and the Exploration of Africa in World History

Richard Worth

Enslow Publishers, Inc.

40 Industrial Road	PO Box 38
Box 398	Aldershot
Berkeley Heights, NJ 07922	Hants GU12 6BP
USA	UK

http://www.enslow.com

Library of Congress Cataloging-in-Publication Data

Worth, Richard.
    Stanley and Livingstone and the exploration of Africa in world history / Richard Worth.
        p. cm. — (In world history)
    Includes bibliographical references (p.) and index.
    Summary: Chronicles the lives and expeditions of Henry Stanley and David Livingstone as they unlocked many geographic secrets of Africa and traces the history of European colonialism on the African continent.
    ISBN 0-7660-1400-2
    1. Stanley, Henry M. (Henry Morton), 1841–1904 Juvenile literature.
2. Livingstone, David, 1813–1873 Juvenile literature. 3. Africa—Discovery and exploration Juvenile literature. [1. Stanley, Henry M. (Henry Morton), 1841–1904. 2. Livingstone, David, 1813–1873. 3. Explorers.
4. Africa—Discovery and exploration.] I. Title. II. Series.
DT351.S6W67 2000
916.704'23'0922 21—dc21
                                       99-39104
                                          CIP

Printed in the United States of America

10 9 8 7 6 5 4 3 2

To Our Readers: We have done our best to make sure all Internet addresses in this book were active and appropriate when we went to press. However, the author and the publisher have no control over and assume no liability for the material available on those Internet sites or on other Web sites they may link to. Any comments or suggestions can be sent by e-mail to comments@enslow.com or to the address on the back cover.

Illustration Credits: Enslow Publishers, Inc., pp. 11, 31, 59, 72, 101, 116; Library of Congress; pp. 8, 15, 22, 25, 33, 42, 44, 47, 53, 54, 61, 66, 68, 83, 89, 91, 93, 103, 106, 111, 117.

Cover Illustration: Library of Congress—Portrait of Henry Morton Stanley; Background—© Digital Vision Ltd.

Contents

Chapter 1

"Dr. Livingstone, I Presume?"

On February 4, 1871, several *dhows*—small Arab sailing ships—left the busy harbor on the island of Zanzibar off the east coast of Africa. They carried a well-armed expedition whose destination was the African interior. The ships were crammed with food, tents, medicines, and cooking utensils for the men. The ships also carried bolts of cotton cloth and bags of colorful beads to be traded with the African tribes to secure safe passage through their territories. Leading the expedition was a thirty-year-old newspaper reporter for the *New York Herald* named Henry Morton Stanley.

What was a reporter doing on his way to the African mainland? According to Stanley, he had been summoned from another assignment covering a war in Spain by James Gordon Bennett, Jr., the *Herald*

James Gordon Bennett, publisher of the New York Herald, *sent Henry Stanley on his first expedition to Africa.*

publisher, who was staying at a luxurious hotel in Paris. When Stanley entered Bennett's room, the publisher told him to sit down, then explained that he had an important project for him. According to Stanley, Bennett said:

> "Where do you think Livingstone is?"
>
> "I really do not know, sir!"
>
> "Do you think he is alive?"
>
> "He may be and he may not be!" [Stanley] answered.
>
> "Well, I think he is alive, and that he can be found, and I am going to send you to find him."
>
> "What!" said [Stanley], "do you really think I can find Dr. Livingstone? Do you mean me to go to Central Africa?"
>
> "Yes; I mean that you shall go, and find him wherever you may hear that he is. . . . Of course you will act according to your own plans, and do what you think best—but find Livingstone!"[1]

Who Was Livingstone?

Dr. David Livingstone was a well-known British explorer and missionary. He had left on an expedition to the African interior in 1866. Since that time, he had not been seen by any outsiders. Livingstone was trying to discover the source of the Nile River, a problem that had perplexed historians and geographers since ancient times. James Gordon Bennett believed that he could create a sensational scoop by sending one of his reporters looking for Livingstone. When the explorer was found, Bennett could splash the headlines across his newspaper and sell thousands of extra copies.

Of course, Livingstone was not really lost. Dr. John Kirk, the British counsel in Zanzibar, periodically sent supplies to drop-off locations so that Livingstone could replenish his expedition. Even Bennett may have realized that he might be trying to create a big story out of nothing. Although he had originally met with Henry Stanley in 1869, Bennett first sent him to the Middle East before instructing him to go to Africa and search for Livingstone. Bennett may have thought that the longer Livingstone remained in the African interior, the more likely it would seem that he needed to be rescued.

During his expedition, Livingstone had pinpointed what he thought was the source of the Nile. The explorer believed that the Nile began as another river that seemed to originate in Lake Bangweolo (located in current-day Zambia). His explorations, however, had left Livingstone weak with illness. In January 1869, he wrote in his journal: "After one hour's march I was too ill to go farther. I had pain in the chest. . . . My lungs were affected. . . . Cannot walk. Pneumonia of the right lung. I cough day and night."[2]

Livingstone had to be carried into Ujiji, an Arab trading town on the eastern shore of Lake Tanganyika (located in present-day Tanzania). There, he hoped to find supplies sent by the British consul. But they had been stolen. There was no food or medicine, and most

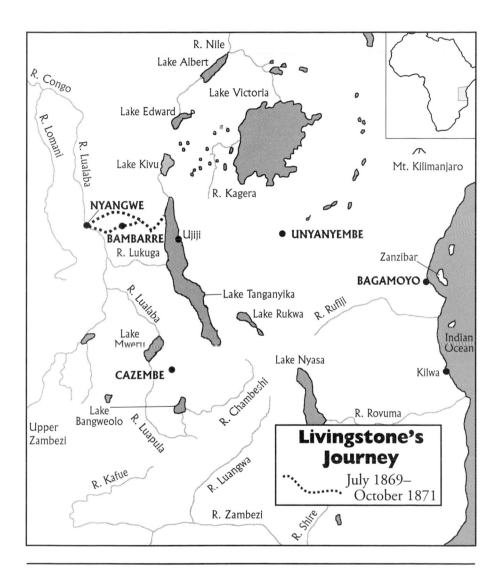

David Livingstone was never really lost. Stanley was hoping to "find" him in order to get a good news story for his newspaper.

of the cloth and beads—which Livingstone might have traded for necessary supplies—were gone, too.

Eventually, Livingstone recuperated at Ujiji. In November, he set out again to confirm his beliefs about the source of the Nile. But illness, combined with the African rainy season and fighting between the Arabs and African tribes over the ivory trade, prevented Livingstone from doing much exploring. He returned to Ujiji in October 1871, only to find that his supplies had been stolen once again. The thief had sold them to buy ivory. Livingstone was near desperation when he received news that a white man was two hundred miles away. Perhaps, Livingstone thought, the man was heading for Ujiji with supplies that might save him.

Stanley's Journey

Henry Stanley's men were singing as they left in March on their mission to locate Livingstone. But the expedition went downhill quickly. Stanley and his men had to struggle through heavy rains that turned the landscape into a swamp, "[W]e splashed, waded, occasionally half-swimming, and reeled through mire," Stanley later wrote.[3]

When some of the Africans on the expedition refused to continue marching, he whipped them repeatedly. He also showed very little sympathy for William Farquhar and John Shaw, his aides on the expedition, who complained constantly about the hardships of the journey and threatened to mutiny.

Indeed, one night Stanley barely escaped being hit by a bullet that cut through his tent. Going outside, he discovered that Shaw's gun barrel was still warm. Shaw claimed that he had dreamed a thief was nearby and shot at him. ". . . I would advise you in future, in order to avoid all suspicion, not to fire into my tent, or at least so near me," Stanley told him.[4]

Stanley also suffered repeatedly from attacks of high fever and dysentery, a severe stomach illness that causes diarrhea and dehydration. But he refused to halt his journey. He sent a steady stream of reports that were printed in the *Herald*, charting his progress.

At one point, however, Stanley's expedition was almost ended by a brutal conflict between an African tribal king and Arab slave traders. Stanley sided with the traders. When they were ambushed, he barely escaped with his life, and most of his men deserted. He was forced to hire new porters to carry his baggage so he could continue the journey. When some of these men later tried to run away, they were dragged back, flogged, and chained. Two of his African guides became so angry with Stanley that they threatened to shoot him. But he would not back down and eventually convinced them to put down their rifles.

By early November, Stanley was nearing Ujiji. He had heard from traders that Livingstone was there. On November 10, Stanley's expedition finally marched into the town, carrying the flags of the United States and Zanzibar and firing guns into the air. There, Stanley came face to face with the man he had been seeking. Although Livingstone was fifty-eight, he looked much older, with his pale features and white beard. Stanley admitted that he was filled with emotion and wanted to hug Livingstone at that moment, but he tried to control himself. He was afraid of how the explorer might react, and wanted to be as dignified as possible. Stanley walked up to Livingstone, took off his hat, and said:

"Dr. Livingstone, I presume?"

"Yes," said he, with a kind smile, lifting his cap slightly.

". . . I thank God, Doctor, I have been permitted to see you."

He answered, "I feel thankful that I am here to welcome you."[5]

Source Document

Well, we are but a mile from Ujiji now, and it is high time we should let them know a caravan is coming; so "Commence firing" is the word passed along the length of the column, and gladly do they begin. . . . The flags are fluttered; the banner of America is in front, waving joyfully; the guide is in the zenith of his glory. . . . Never were the Stars and Stripes so beautiful to my mind—the breeze of the Tanganyika has such an effect on them.[6]

Stanley later wrote about his trip to find Dr. Livingstone.

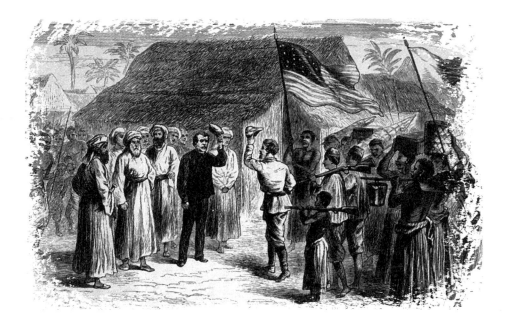

An artist drew this illustration of Henry Stanley's meeting with David Livingstone in Africa.

Through Stanley's dispatches, the *New York Herald* trumpeted the story of this fateful meeting to its readers. Millions of others read about it in newspapers across Europe. Bennett would later telegraph Stanley that he was world famous. But even more important, European nations would begin focusing their attention on Africa. Over the next three decades, they would carve the entire continent into colonies.

Chapter 2

Dr. Livingstone in Africa

David Livingstone was born in Blantyre, Scotland, eight miles from the city of Glasgow, on March 19, 1813. David's father, Neil Livingstone, was a tea salesman. He earned so little money that his family of seven children was forced to live in a tiny, cramped apartment in a run-down tenement building. But Neil Livingstone did not believe that a man's success was measured only by his material possessions. He had a strong religious faith. During his sales trips, he distributed pamphlets that preached the word of God.

When David was ten, he went to work in a cotton mill. Child labor was quite common in England during this period. Many poor families depended on the extra money their children could earn by working in the factories. David worked a fourteen-hour day, six days a week. He often picked up an odd job on Sundays as well on one of the farms outside Blantyre. It was an exhausting schedule. Still, a few children somehow found enough energy to attend the company school in the evenings after work. David was one of them. He developed a keen interest in natural science. He would spend his free time identifying rocks and gathering plant specimens in the countryside.

It was almost unheard of that a boy of David's poor circumstances would aspire to become a doctor—a career that required college training and the money to pay for it. Yet David was determined to succeed. He saved money and mastered the basics of science and math. At the age of twenty-three, he was admitted to Anderson's College in Glasgow.

Filled with his father's deep religious faith, David decided to combine medicine with missionary work. This would enable him to save the souls as well as the bodies of people thousands of miles away in China, Africa, or South America. While he was still in medical school, David Livingstone applied to the London Missionary Society. In 1840, after completing medical school and theological (religious) training, he was sent to South Africa. There, Great Britain had established the thriving Cape Colony. He was assigned to work with Robert Moffat, a famous missionary who had established a mission at Kuruman.

Livingstone Starts His Missionary Work

Livingstone had attended a lecture given by Moffat in England in which he glowingly described the large

Source Document

My reading while at work was carried on by placing the book on a portion of the spinning-jenny, so that I could catch sentence after sentence as I passed at my work; I thus kept up a pretty constant study undisturbed by the roar of the machinery.

To this part of my education I owe my present power of completely abstracting the mind from surrounding noises, so as to read and write with perfect comfort amid the play of children or near the dancing and songs of savages.

The toil of cotton-spinning, to which I was promoted in my nineteenth year, was excessively severe on a slim, loose-jointed lad, but it was well paid for; and it enabled me to support myself while attending medical and Greek classes in Glasgow in winter, as also the divinity lectures of Dr. Wardlaw, by working with my hands in summer. I never received a farthing of aid from any one, and should have accomplished my project of going to China as a medical missionary, in the course of time, by my own efforts, had not some friends advised my joining the London Missionary Society on account of its perfectly unsectarian character. It "sends neither Episcopacy, nor Presbyterianism, nor Independency, but the Gospel of Christ to the heathen." This exactly agreed with my ideas of what a missionary society ought to do; but it was not without a pang that I offered myself, for it was not quite agreeable to one accustomed to work his own way to become in a measure dependent on others; and I would not have been much put about though my offer had been rejected.[1]

In his later writings about his explorations, Livingstone included brief mentions of his early life, such as this description of his love of reading and his eagerness to become a missionary.

mission he had created among the Africans. This may have been one of the reasons that Livingstone wanted to go there. He arrived in Cape Town, South Africa, in March 1841. Livingstone then began the trek of approximately six hundred miles from the coast through the stark African wilderness that would bring him to Kuruman in Bechuanaland.

What he saw on his arrival sadly disappointed him. "All around is a dreary desert for a great part of the year," he wrote. "There is not a tree near the station which has not been planted by the missionaries. Low stunted scraggy bushes, many of them armed with bent thorns villainously sharp and strong are the chief objects which present themselves to the eye."[2]

Moffat had worked at his mission for twenty years, winning far more converts than many other missionaries. But the number was still very small. For centuries, the Africans had practiced ancestor worship, believed in witchcraft, and embraced polygamy (marriage to multiple wives)—all practices that the missionaries tried to eliminate. But few Africans saw any reason to give up their customs and religious beliefs to adopt Western culture and Christianity. Polygamy, for example, made perfect sense in a culture where the number of children a man had was a measure of his influence in the tribe. Because women were the farmers in a village, multiple wives would also enable a man to grow more food and throw larger social gatherings to impress his neighbors.

However, the most evil practice in Africa, at least in the minds of the missionaries, was slavery. In 1833, Great Britain had abolished slavery throughout its empire, which included South Africa. But in many parts of the continent, the practice continued.

The Portuguese engaged in slavery in their colonies of Angola on the west coast of Africa and Mozambique on the east coast. Zanzibar was a center of the ivory and slave trade under its Arab ruler Sayyid Said. The African tribes often acted as middlemen for the slave trade, selling the people they conquered into slavery in return for cloth, beads, and guns from the Arabs and Europeans. Indeed, one of the only reasons the Africans accepted missionaries among them was that they could fix the guns that often broke after the Africans used them.

These were the conditions that Robert Moffat had faced during his two decades in Africa. Now, David Livingstone would have to deal with them, too.

Establishing His Own Mission

Although Livingstone spent a couple of years at Kuruman, he did not intend to work forever in Moffat's shadow. He preferred to be in charge of his own mission. Soon after his arrival, he was already traveling north with another missionary to find a site for a new post.

It was a tough journey, undertaken during the terrible heat of the African summer. Along the way, Livingstone tried preaching the gospel to the people

Dr. David Livingstone worked as a missionary before becoming an African explorer.

he encountered. They seemed to have very little interest in Christianity.

While he was establishing a new mission at Mabotsa in Bechuanaland in 1843 and 1844, Livingstone tried to help several Africans chase away a lion that had taken some of their sheep. Carefully aiming his gun, he fired at the creature but merely wounded it. This barely slowed the lion, and it came charging toward him. In an effort to protect himself, Livingstone put up his arm, only to feel the lion's powerful teeth tear through the skin and crush the bone. Livingstone might easily have been killed if one of the Africans had not reacted very quickly and fired at the lion, finally killing it.

Married Life and New Missions

Livingstone took several weeks to recover from this injury. After his recuperation, he journeyed south to visit with the Moffats. During the time he had worked at Kuruman, Livingstone had developed a relationship with Mary, one of the Moffats' daughters. In 1845, they were married.

The Livingstones spent very little time at the mission in Mabotsa. He and the other missionary had a heated disagreement over who should get the credit for establishing the new mission. The Livingstones left Mabotsa and established new missions, first at Chonwane—forty miles to the north—in 1845, and two years later at Kolobeng, another forty miles northwest. Livingstone had been invited to Chonwane by a tribal chief named Sechele. There, the Livingstones established a home, a chapel, and a school. Sechele learned to read English and even dressed in European clothes. But neither the chief nor any of the members of his tribe embraced Christianity.

A terrible drought finally persuaded the Livingstone family to establish the second mission, at Kolobeng, which was also located in Sechele's territory. There, the Livingstones led a simple life of hard work and family time:

> The Livingstones usually got up at dawn, had family prayers, breakfast and then school for anybody prepared to come. The rest of the morning Livingstone devoted to manual work—sawing, ploughing, smithy work and anything else that needed doing. Mary would spend her morning cooking, sewing and looking after the children. Lunch would be followed by a short rest, and after that . . . Livingstone went on with his manual tasks till about five o'clock. After that he generally . . . milked the cows, and finally went to the chief's house to pray and give him special instruction.[3]

The Livingstones and their mission were finally successful in encouraging Sechele to convert to Christianity, but he was the only member of his tribe who did. Meanwhile, drought struck again and the Livingstones lost their crops. Kolobeng had been no more successful than their first mission.

Family was an important part of Livingstone's life. David Livingstone posed for this photograph with his young daughter.

The First Expeditions

Determination was one of David Livingstone's outstanding characteristics. It had enabled him to escape the slums of Blantyre and become a missionary doctor against enormous odds. Now his determination propelled Livingstone, who had already established missions farther north in Africa than any other Englishman, to push even farther into the African frontier.

Livingstone had heard about a lake to the north that no European had ever visited. Livingstone wanted to be the first to explore it and perhaps establish a site for another mission. Livingstone, however, could not afford to buy supplies and hire porters, which such an expedition would require. Fortunately, while he was still at Mabotsa, he had met a well-to-do Englishman named William Cotton Oswell, who was game hunting in the area. Oswell not only agreed to finance the expedition to see the lake, but also accompanied Livingstone on his journey north from June to October 1849.

In order to reach the lake, Livingstone and Oswell had to cross the great Kalahari Desert, whose reddish sands stretch for more than one hundred thousand square miles. Most of the time, the brutally hot and dry desert was far too dangerous for travelers to cross. At certain times of the year, however, the Kalahari receives rain, which makes possible an expedition across the desert to the north. In this rainy season, Livingstone found that the country through which they traveled was "covered with bushes and trees . . . with lilac flowers." They also found water in a few hollows to supply their horses and oxen:

> By the aid of spades and fingers, two of the holes were cleared out so as to form pits six feet deep and about as many broad. Our guides were earnest in their injunctions not to break through the hard crust of sand at the bottom, in which case "the water would go away." . . . Enough water accumulated for the horses that evening. . . . Next morning we found the water had flowed in faster than at first. . . . The supply, which at the beginning was only enough for a few men, becomes in a few days sufficient for the oxen as well.[4]

After a trip of three hundred miles, Livingstone reached Lake Ngami (located in the modern nation of Botswana). On August 1, 1849, he and his expedition stood on the northeast end of the lake and became the first white Europeans to see it.

In 1851, Livingstone and Oswell journeyed north again. This time, they hoped to reach the Zambesi River, which originates in central Africa and flows for approximately seventeen hundred miles to the western coast. Livingstone finally reached the Zambesi on August 4, 1851. He believed incorrectly that he was the first European to do so. (A Portuguese explorer had been there ahead of him.) Livingstone was accompanied by his wife and children on this expedition. They hoped to establish themselves in a new mission among the Makololo, who inhabited an area along the Zambesi.

Upon his arrival, Livingstone was very unhappy to discover that the Makololo were engaged in the slave trade. However, he believed that the Zambesi River and his mission there might end that problem. Livingstone was one of the only missionaries who believed that Christianity and commerce must work hand in hand if there was any chance of changing the customs of the African people. He hoped European traders might sail along the Zambesi, bringing beads and cloth in exchange for the ivory tusks the Africans harvested from elephants. Ivory was in great demand in Europe for piano and organ keys as well as for furniture handles and figurines. This commerce might eliminate the need for the Africans to engage in the slave trade. Also, as they learned about European commerce, the Africans might be persuaded to adopt other European customs, give up their traditional ways, and embrace Christianity. It was a bold vision— one that would drive Livingstone to undertake many more explorations in Africa.

Traveling Across the Continent

In 1852, Dr. Livingstone and his family returned to Cape Town. While they had been in the north, his children had contracted malaria. This disease is carried by the anopheles mosquito that breeds in warm, swampy areas. Malaria can be fatal unless it is treated. Fortunately, Livingstone had a drug called quinine, which is used to treat the disease. Nevertheless, Livingstone knew his expeditions might prove unsafe for his family. He put them on a ship headed back to England, where they went to live with his parents.

The following year, Livingstone returned to the land of the Makololo. He was forced to cross the flooded Chobe River. The trip became so difficult that most of his porters deserted him. With only one man, Livingstone continued his journey. "Vallies appeared like large deep rivers, with hippopotami in them," he wrote:

> We waded among reed and high grass for three days, trying to obtain a passage in to the Chobe through the dense masses of reed . . . which line its banks. On the fourth day we attained our object, launched the . . . [boat], and after passing along about 20 miles we reached a Makololo village. In their figurative language they said I "had come down upon them as if I had dropped out of a cloud. . . ."[5]

The Makololo were clearly astounded that anyone could have survived such an ordeal.

Livingstone did not remain at Linyanti, the capital of the Makololo, for very long. First, he embarked on a brief journey northwest, up the Zambesi. Because Linyanti was afflicted with malaria, he hoped to find a site for a new mission and trading station that would be safe from the disease. He was unsuccessful. In November 1853, Livingstone began another expedition to find a route traders could follow into the African interior.

The first leg of his journey took Livingstone along the Zambesi, then west to the African coast—a trip of more than a thousand miles. The Makololo chief had given him a few porters, a little food, and a small supply of trade goods to barter for any supplies he might need along the way.

Each day, Livingstone and his men would begin their travel early in the morning. By midday, the heat was almost intolerable. Nevertheless, Livingstone always had time to take note of the beauty he saw along the Zambesi—different varieties of flowers, lush trees, and all types of animal life. "The ground swarms with insect life," he wrote, "and in the cool mornings . . . rings with the singing of birds. . . . The notes . . . strike the mind by their boldness and variety as the wellings forth from joyous hearts of praise to Him who fills them with overflowing gladness."[6]

Eventually, Livingstone left the Zambesi and headed overland. His party slogged through the mud created by the African rainy season with little to eat. Their supplies had run out, and they had few items to trade. At one point, they were surrounded and threatened by a fierce people called the Chiboque. "Our crime consisted in one of our men, when spitting, allowing a small drop of the saliva to fall on one of them. I replied," Livingstone wrote, "if the chief could seriously say such was a crime I was willing to pay a fine." He offered them something, but the Chiboque turned it down. Fortunately, Livingstone and his men were carrying enough guns to frighten the Chiboque. Eventually, they agreed to a peace offering—an ox.[7] As the hardships of the trip

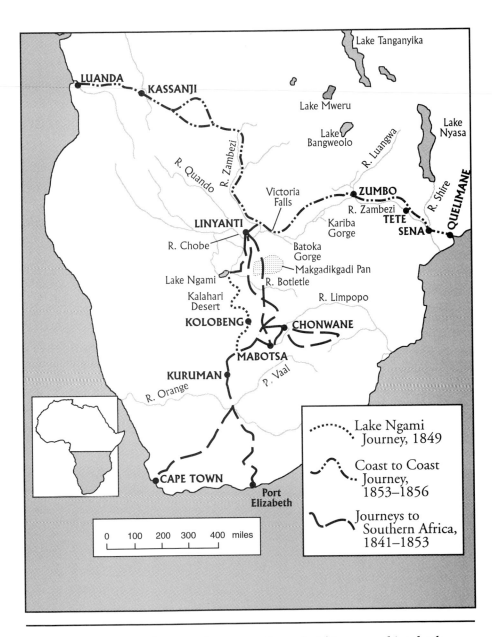

Livingstone made several voyages through Africa, searching both
for new geographical information and for a place to start a mission.

continued, Livingstone's men wanted to abandon the expedition. He could prevent them from leaving only by threatening to shoot them. On May 1, 1854, Livingstone finally reached the Portuguese settlement at Luanda on the coast. He had been suffering from malaria during much of the trip. Because someone had stolen his medicine, he barely survived.

Once in Luanda, Livingstone was treated successfully. But in light of the difficulty of his trip, he realized that the route would be unsuitable for trading. Undaunted by his illness, he headed back to Linyanti, gathered porters and supplies, and began heading along the Zambesi to the east.

". . . [W]e came in sight, for the first time, of the columns of vapour appropriately called 'smoke,' rising at a distance of five miles, exactly as when large tracts of grass are burned in Africa."[8] This vapor came from giant waterfalls, which Livingstone named after Queen Victoria, the British monarch. In November 1855, he became the first European to see them. Victoria Falls are formed when the Zambesi drops through a 420-foot-deep chasm. North of the falls, Livingstone also found the broad Batoka Plateau. He believed this area might be a good place for Europeans to raise cattle and set up a trading post. He also thought he might establish a mission there. Merchants could sail to the falls from the east coast, then head to the plateau, creating a viable trade route.

Livingstone now hurried eastward, heading overland for a distance to shorten his trip, then rejoining

Victoria Falls

Source Document

I resolved on the following day to visit the falls of Victoria, called by the natives Mosioatunya, or more anciently Shongwe. Of these we had often heard since we came into the country: indeed one of the questions asked by Sebituane was "Have you smoke that sounds in your country?" They did not go near enough to examine them, but, viewing them with awe at a distance, said, in reference to the vapour and noise, "Mosi oa tunya" (smoke does sound there). . . . I . . . gave the only English name I have affixed to any part of the country. . . .[9]

David Livingstone wrote about his experience in becoming the first white European to see Victoria Falls.

the Zambesi again until he had reached the coast at Quelimane. He had become the first European to cross the continent. By the time he arrived in England, word of his travels had preceded him. Livingstone was hailed as a great hero. He enjoyed the fame success had given him.

In 1857, he published his book, *Missionary Travels and Researches in South Africa*. It became an instant best-seller in England. Europeans learned much about the geography of the African continent. Many were surprised to learn from Livingstone's book that it was not a vast desert but contained broad rivers, lush forests, and a variety of wildlife.

Livingstone also spoke to large audiences. He asked them to join him in his important work and complete it even if he were unable to: "I direct your attention to Africa. I know that in a few years I shall be cut off in that country which is now open. I go back to try to open up a path to Commerce and Christianity. Do you carry on the work that I have begun. I leave it to you."[10]

Back to Africa

Livingstone's interest in establishing a trading colony in central Africa had taken him far away from the goals of the London Missionary Society. While home in England, Livingstone left the society and accepted a position from the British government as a representative in Africa. He also received funding for another expedition of the Zambesi. European nations at this time were very interested in finding new opportunities for investment. Control and development of colonies in Africa would provide just the kind of opportunities Europe was looking for. For this reason, exploration was encouraged and funded.

Livingstone returned to Africa in 1858, accompanied by his wife, Mary. He hoped to prove that the Zambesi was navigable to a point near the Batoka Plateau.

This time, he sailed along the river in a small steamship called the *Ma-Robert*, the name the Makololo had given Mary Livingstone—the mother of Robert, the couple's oldest son. It was a difficult journey. The river was low and the ship often ran aground. The ship had not been built to carry heavy loads of supplies, and its engine did not run efficiently. It consumed enormous amounts of wood fuel.

In addition, many of the men on the expedition, who had come to Africa for the first time, contracted malaria. Livingstone showed little sympathy for their suffering, however, and kept the expedition moving forward. Unfortunately, the *Ma-Robert* then encountered an obstacle that even Livingstone, with all his determination, could not overcome: the Kebrabasa Rapids.

He had missed the rapids on his journey in 1855–1856 because he had taken an overland route part of the way. At one point, the water in the rapids plummeted thirty feet from one level to another. Livingstone examined the rapids three times. He was reluctant, at first, to give up his dream of turning the Zambesi into a trade route. But it was impossible for any ship to go through the treacherous rapids.

Searching for an Alternate Site

In 1859, Livingstone explored another area that he hoped might serve as a trading colony in Africa. This was the river Shire, which connected with the Zambesi east of the Kebrabasa Rapids. During his first expeditions in the early months of the year, Livingstone and his men met hostile warriors who fired poisoned arrows at them. Eventually, their journey was stopped by a series of rapids that ran for thirty miles and could not be crossed. Livingstone left the river and headed north toward the Shire highlands. It seemed to be an area free of malaria that might serve as a suitable colony. He also reached Lake Nyasa.

Unfortunately, the highlands and Lake Nyasa regions were being torn apart by war. This was also a center for the slave trade. Nevertheless, Livingstone downplayed the risks involved in colonizing the area. He tried to convince the British government in London that the problems could be solved:

> By means of a small steamer, purchasing the ivory of the lake and river above the cataracts, . . . the slave-trade in this quarter would be rendered unprofitable; for it is only by the ivory being carried by the slaves [instead of paid porters] that the latter do not eat up all the profits of a trip . . . and if we could give them the same prices which they at present get after carrying their merchandise 300 miles beyond this to the Coast, it might induce them to return without going further. It is only by cutting off the supplies in the interior that we can crush the slave-trade on the Coast.[11]

A permanent English presence in the area backed by an armed steamer, Livingstone hoped, might eventually lead to settlements and missionary posts.

Mission in the Highlands

Before any ships could be put on the lake, however, a group of missionaries, led by the bishop of Cape Town, decided to establish an outpost in the Shire highlands. They had been encouraged to come there by Livingstone. In 1861, as Livingstone and the missionaries journeyed to the area, they encountered traders leading a large group of slaves. Upon seeing the English, they ran off, leaving the slaves behind. "They were thus left entirely in our hands," Livingstone wrote,

> and knives were soon busy at work cutting the women and children loose. It was more difficult to cut the men adrift, as each had his neck in the fork of a stout stick, six or seven feet long, and kept in by an iron rod which was riveted at both ends across the throat. With a saw, luckily in the bishop's baggage, one by one the men were sawn out into freedom.[12]

It was an eye-opening and harsh introduction to the area for the missionaries, but their situation would only grow worse. While Livingstone left the missionaries so that he could explore Lake Nyasa on his own, the tribal wars continued around them. The bishop of Cape Town became sick and died, and a number of the other missionaries eventually succumbed to malaria. Meanwhile, Livingstone's wife, Mary, also contracted the disease. She died in 1862.

Dr. David Livingstone wanted very much to continue his expeditions through the African continent. However, drought, the deaths of the missionaries, an outbreak of fever among Livingstone's men, and the men's unwillingness to endure any further hardships forced Livingstone to bring his efforts to a close. In 1863, he returned to England. He had failed to achieve his goals of bringing European commerce and Christianity to Africa.

Chapter 3

Who Was
Henry Stanley?

In the town of Denbigh, Wales, a nineteen-year-old servant girl named Betsy Parry gave birth to an illegitimate son on January 28, 1841. She called him John Rowlands, after his father. Two decades later, John became Henry Stanley. Eventually, he would be acclaimed as one of the greatest explorers of the nineteenth century.

These remarkable events began when John was still a baby. His mother decided that she could not keep him. Betsy gave the child to her father, Moses Parry, a farmer. John was well cared for until he was five. Then, his grandfather died suddenly while working in the fields. The boy's uncles placed him in foster care.

When the foster family could no longer afford his upkeep, their son Dick took John to the St. Asaph

Union Workhouse outside of Denbigh. Workhouses were the final destination for the poor and the elderly in nineteenth-century Great Britain when no one wanted them. As John was taken away from his foster family and led to the workhouse door, Dick kept assuring the sad little boy that his stay would be only temporary. It was a lie.

Years later, Stanley wrote,

> Though forty-five years have passed since that dreadful evening, my resentment has not a whit abated. Dick's guile was well meant, no doubt, but I then learned for the first time that one's professed friend can smile while preparing to deal a mortal blow, and that a man can mask evil with a show of goodness.

The event, he continued, succeeded in "shattering my confidence and planting the first seeds of distrust in a child's heart."[1]

While he lived at the workhouse with other poor children like him, John received an education designed to prepare him for a trade. He was taught by a schoolmaster named James Francis. Like many other teachers of that era, Francis was a brutal man who did not hesitate to use a stick or a whip to enforce discipline. Under Francis's watchful eye, John learned reading, writing, and arithmetic while developing an early interest in geography. But at fifteen, John decided that it was time for him to see what lay outside the walls of St. Asaph's. So he left.

John Rowlands, as he looked during his teenage years.

At first, John hoped he might receive some help from relatives, but each one, in turn, showed little interest in him. Eventually, he went to live with his aunt Mary, who owned a general store and tavern. She soon sent him off to an uncle named Tom Morris in Liverpool, a large port city in central England. Unfortunately, Uncle Tom and his family were down on their luck. They had hoped to find John a job, but when this did not occur, his aunt was forced to take a more dire alternative. Stanley remembered: "On Monday morning of the next week she borrowed my . . . suit, and took it to the place of the three gilt balls [the pawn shop]. The Monday after, she took my overcoat to the same place, and then I knew that the family was in great trouble."[2]

Eventually, John found a job with a butcher shop on the Liverpool docks. One of his responsibilities was delivering food to some of the ships at anchor. One day, when he was visiting a packet ship named the *Windemere*, the captain asked if he would like to join the crew and go to America. Although John knew nothing about being a sailor, he decided to go. After a seven-week voyage, John arrived in New Orleans, Louisiana.

Life in America

In February 1859, John Rowlands walked down Tchoupitoulas Street along the New Orleans waterfront. He had entered one of the world's busiest seaports. Cotton was shipped from Southern

The port of New Orleans, as it looked at the time young John Rowlands arrived in America.

plantations down the Mississippi River and stacked on the wharves in New Orleans. Later, it would be transported in large sailing vessels to mills in New England or in Great Britain, where it was made into cloth. Goods such as coffee, crystal glassware, and fine china arrived in New Orleans from the Caribbean and Europe.

As John walked down the street, he came to the doorway of an office named Speake and McCreary, where he saw a man reading a newspaper. Having decided to leave the ship, John asked the man for a job. First, the man wanted to know if John could read. Stanley later wrote, "he pointed to an article in his newspaper, and said, 'Read that.' It was something about a legislative assembly, which I delivered, as he said, 'very correctly, but with an un-American accent.'" Then he asked John whether he could write. "Yes, sir," was the answer, but the man wanted to make sure. "'Then let me see you mark that coffee-sack, with the same address you see on the one near it. There is the marking-pot and brush.'"[3]

This was John Rowlands's introduction to Henry Stanley, an Englishman who had come to America many years earlier and become a successful merchant. When Stanley was completely satisfied with John's clerical skills, he introduced him to the firm's owner. John was hired as a junior clerk.

Gradually, the relationship between John and Henry Stanley deepened. John was invited to Stanley's home for breakfast and met his wife, Frances. Many other visits followed. For John Rowlands, Stanley not only became a friend and teacher, but the father he had never known. Stanley even offered to adopt John, but soon after the adoption occurred, Stanley died in Cuba while on a business trip.

At least, this is the version that John Rowlands, who soon began calling himself Henry Stanley, told in his autobiography. However, John Bierman, a Stanley biographer, believes that this story is not true. According to Bierman, "The lad [John Rowlands] wanted more than a benefactor; he wanted a family, but that was not on offer."[4] Bierman's research shows that Henry Stanley, the merchant, lived until 1878, and that there probably was no adoption at all. The merchant most likely found John's desire for a family more than he could handle and moved him out of New Orleans to a new position in Arkansas. There, early in 1861, John went to work at a country store.

The Civil War

When John Rowlands, now calling himself Henry Stanley, reached Arkansas, the dark clouds of civil war were already beginning to form. One by one, the Southern states, including Arkansas, left the Union and joined the Confederacy. In Cyprus Bend, where Stanley was working, his friends enlisted in a regiment known as the Dixie Greys. Although he was not a Southerner, Stanley felt pressured to volunteer with the other young men.

He fought his first major battle at Shiloh in 1862. The Confederate Army, commanded by General Albert Sidney Johnston, surprised the Union forces at dawn on April 6. Stanley recalled:

> After a steady exchange of musketry, which lasted some time, we heard the order: "Fix Bayonets! On the double-quick!" in tones that thrilled us. There was a simultaneous bound forward, each soul doing his best for the emergency. The Federals [Union soldiers] appeared inclined to await us; but, at this juncture, our men raised a yell, thousands responded to it, and burst out into the wildest yelling it has ever been my lot to hear.[5]

The Battle of Shiloh, one of the bloodiest of the Civil War.

At the sound of the rebel yell, the Union troops began to retreat. By the end of the first day, they had been pushed back almost into the Tennessee River.

The cost in both Northern and Southern lives was appalling. Stanley described men lying in pools of their own sticky blood. The following day, the tide of battle began moving against the Confederates, and Stanley became separated from the other members of the Dixie Greys. Suddenly, Stanley remembered, "I found myself a solitary grey, in a line of blue skirmishers! My companions had retreated! The next I heard was, 'Down with that gun, . . .'" He was a prisoner.[6]

Stanley was taken to a prison camp outside of Chicago. There, men were packed together in such terrible conditions that many died of disease. He eventually realized that the only way out of prison was to join the Union Army. But before he could see any action, Stanley was stricken with illness himself and left the army.

He returned to England briefly, then sailed back to America, where he believed there were more opportunities for him. After a Union victory ended the Civil War, Stanley obtained a job as a reporter for the *Missouri Democrat*. He traveled to cities such as Denver and San Francisco, sending back stories on what he found there. In 1867, he covered the battles the United States Army was fighting against the Plains Indians, who were trying to prevent white settlers from moving into their lands. In order to add to his income, Stanley sold some of his stories to the *New York Herald*, published by James Gordon Bennett, Jr.

A Job With the *Herald*

After covering the war against the Plains Indians, Stanley decided to go east and find a job in New York. There, newspapers such as the *Herald*, the *Tribune*, and the *Times* were considered prestigious places to work for any young journalist. Although he was still a young reporter, he brazenly requested an interview with the arrogant Bennett, who agreed to see him.

Stanley told the publisher that he wanted to cover a war that was currently going on in Abyssinia (present-day Ethiopia) on the east coast of Africa. Bennett did not believe that this conflict would be very interesting to most Americans. But if Stanley would agree to pay his own expenses, Bennett said, he would hire him as a freelance reporter and pay him for any stories that were printed in the *Herald*.

The War in Abyssinia

The deal was good enough for Stanley. He left for the Middle East at the end of 1867. Stanley arrived at Suez, in northeastern Egypt, where a giant canal was being built that would connect the Mediterranean Sea with the Red Sea. Telegraph offices were also located in Suez. Any reporter covering the war in Abyssinia would have to send out his stories via telegraph so they would reach the *Herald*'s offices in Europe. To make sure his stories got there ahead of the competition, Stanley paid a clerk in the telegraph office. Then, he headed south to Abyssinia.

There, the British were about to defeat an army of African troops led by their king, Theodore. Relying on superior weapons, the British slaughtered hundreds of Abyssinians. King Theodore eventually committed suicide. As soon as the war ended, Stanley rushed to the coast and boarded a ship so he could sail back to Suez with his story. When the ship finally arrived, it was unable to dock immediately. But Stanley somehow figured out a way to get his report to the clerk at the telegraph office. It was the first newspaper story to be sent to Europe. As it turned out, communication lines from Egypt were interrupted immediately afterward. Stanley had a scoop.

Covering the War in Spain

After the war in Abyssinia, Stanley found himself covering another conflict—this time in Spain. From his balcony in Saragossa, a city in northern Spain, he watched the battle between the rebels and the government troops. "As the bullets flattened themselves with a dull thud against the balcony where I stood," he wrote, "I sought the shelter of the roof, and . . . I observed the desperate fighting."[7] The battle see-sawed until the government troops finally retreated.

The war in Spain continued, but Stanley was not there to cover its conclusion. In the fall of 1869, James Gordon Bennett called him to Paris for the meeting that would send him in search of David Livingstone.

Chapter 4

Stanley and Livingstone

In 1864, Livingstone had come back to England after the failure of his expeditions and the deaths of the missionaries. Many people in Great Britain criticized him. They had lost faith in him as an experienced explorer and in his ability to open up the African continent. But Livingstone would have one more opportunity to redeem himself. In 1865, he was commissioned by England's Royal Geographic Society, an organization that promoted exploration, to find the source of the Nile.

Seeking the Source of the Nile

The Nile is the world's longest river. One of the earliest civilizations—ancient Egypt—arose along the banks of this mighty river. Its annual floods create a narrow strip of fertile land in the midst of the desert.

This allows crops to grow and support a flourishing culture. The Nile, which flows northward for more than four thousand miles, empties into the Mediterranean Sea. The river originates in central Africa, but for centuries, geographers were uncertain where the source of the Nile might be.

In 1858, an expedition led by British explorers Richard Burton and John Speke became the first Europeans to reach the shores of Lake Tanganyika. At the time, some experts believed the lake was the Nile's source. Then, in 1862, Speke, traveling north of Lake Tanganyika along Lake Victoria—Africa's largest lake—discovered that water was flowing out of the lake's northern side. Speke was convinced that he had found the headwaters of the Nile. But a short time later, Samuel White Baker announced that Speke was wrong. While exploring a body of water that he called Lake Albert—west of Lake Victoria—Baker believed he had found the origin of the Nile.

Livingstone, however, was convinced that these explorers were wrong. He believed that the Nile began much farther south in a small lake called Bangweolo. Livingstone hoped to prove that he was right by going to Lake Bangweolo and tracing the river northward.

Return to Africa

Livingstone arrived in Zanzibar in 1866. For the next five years, he would try to prove that his theories about the origin of the Nile were correct. According to biographer Tim Jeal, the explorer was trying to

Sir Richard Burton was one of the first two Europeans to see Lake Tanganyika.

Captain John Speke (left) believed he had found the source of the Nile River in Lake Victoria. James Grant (right) had been on Speke's expedition.

accomplish something else, as well. The area he would be exploring was also the center of the Arab slave trade. With his deep religious convictions, Livingstone regarded slavery as a tremendous evil in Africa. By exposing the slave trade, he hoped to persuade the British government to move in and try to eliminate it. As Jeal explained, "in time it would be hard to judge whether the search for the Nile's source or [Livingstone's] desire to expose the slave-trade was his dominant motive."[1]

During his expeditions, Livingstone found plenty of evidence that the slave trade was flourishing. He also saw how cruelly the traders treated their victims. "We passed a woman tied by the neck to a tree, and dead," he wrote:

> The people of the country explained that she had been unable to keep up with the other slaves in a gang, and her master had determined that she should not become the property of anyone else, if she recovered after resting for a time. I may say that we saw others tied in a similar manner. The explanation we invariably got was that the Arab, who owned these victims, was enraged at losing his money by the slaves being unable to walk, and gave vent to his spleen by murdering them.[2]

In July 1871, Livingstone was resting at the town of Nyangwe on the Lualaba River. Suddenly, an argument broke out between an African and several armed Arabs, probably slave traders. Before Livingstone realized it, shooting had begun. People fled from the center of the village and desperately tried to reach the river. They hoped to escape in canoes, but there were too many of them. They became jammed together in the river. Already wounded by the Arabs' firing into the crowd, men and women leapt into the river. "Most of these would inevitably drown," Livingstone wrote. "Shot after shot continued to be fired on the helpless and perishing. Some of the long line of heads disappeared quietly. . . ." About four hundred people died.[3]

Livingstone left Nyangwe and went back to Ujiji. It was there Stanley found him ill in November. Livingstone recovered quickly with the food and medicine that Stanley had brought. The journalist wrote that Livingstone kept repeating, "You have brought me new life."[4]

During the days they spent in Ujiji, the explorer and the journalist developed a close personal relationship. Stanley was very impressed with what Livingstone had accomplished. In his reports, Stanley painted Livingstone as a hero. Stanley listened closely as Livingstone poured out the details of his explorations with those "lips that cannot lie." He wrote:

> Dr. Livingstone is a truly pious man—a man deeply imbued with real religious instincts. . . . There is another point in Livingstone's character about which we, as readers of his books and students of his travels, would naturally wish to know something . . . his ability to withstand the rigors of an African climate, and the constant energy with which he follows the exploration of Central Africa.

Stanley then added: "After this study of him I cannot better sum up his character than by using the words of one of my own men: 'He is a good man, an extremely good and kind man.'"[5]

An African Journey Together

John Bierman, a Stanley biographer, believed that Stanley finally found in Livingstone the father he had never known.[6] He raised the explorer's fame to new heights throughout Europe and America. In November, the two men headed north to explore Lake Tanganyika. Along the way, their canoe had to dodge large hippopotami that might capsize a boat, killing the men inside it.

African villages lay along the shores of the lake. At one point, the members of the expedition were forced to pay tribute to a local tribe. At another, a tribe hurled stones at them. Stanley suffered from bouts of malarial fever during the trip. "But though this fever," he wrote, "was more severe than usual, I did not much regret its occurrence, since I became the recipient of the very tender and fatherly kindness of the good man whose companion I now found myself."[7] In earlier journeys, Livingstone had shown very little tolerance of those who could not keep going—as he could—even with a high fever. He treated Stanley far differently.

Livingstone's Final Journey

After their expedition on Lake Tanganyika, Stanley and Livingstone returned to Ujiji. Then they embarked on a journey that would take them eastward toward the coast. Stanley intended to return to Europe. Livingstone would remain at Tabora, part way to the coast, where Stanley would send him porters. Livingstone needed them to continue his expedition to confirm the location of the Nile's source.

When the time came to say good-bye, Livingstone and Stanley were saddened to leave each other. "We had a sad breakfast together," Stanley wrote later. "I could not eat, my heart was too full; neither did my companion seem to have an appetite."[8] Livingstone had even suggested that Stanley come along on the expedition to Lake Bangweolo. This was unusual. Livingstone was a loner who usually liked to lead expeditions by himself in order to become the first to make any new discoveries. Stanley, however, decided to return to Europe.

Livingstone remained in Tabora for several months. In August 1872, after the porters arrived, he began his trip to Lake Bangweolo. Although his health had improved when he was traveling with Stanley, Livingstone now grew ill again. The heat was intense; then the rains came, forcing his expedition to move very slowly. Now fifty-nine, Livingstone's long years of traveling in Africa had taken a tremendous toll on him. The man who seemed capable of making his way through any type of terrain now had to be carried across the swollen rivers. He also had doubts about whether his theories were correct. He had believed the Luapula became the Lualaba River, which he thought flowed into the Nile. But Livingstone began to wonder

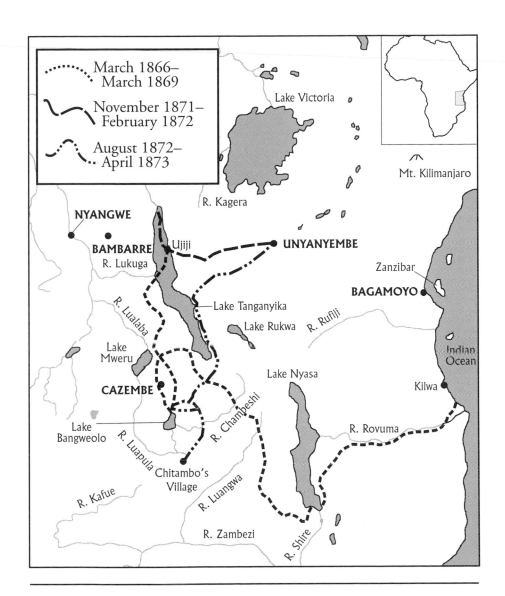

Lake Victoria

Mt. Kilimanjaro

R. Kagera

NYANGWE

BAMBARRE
R. Lukuga

Ujiji

UNYANYEMBE

Zanzibar

BAGAMOYO

R. Lualaba

Lake Tanganyika

Lake Rukwa

R. Rufiji

Lake
Mweru

CAZEMBE

Lake Nyasa

Indian
Ocean

Kilwa

Lake
Bangweolo

R. Luapula

R. Chambeshi

Chitambo's
Village

R. Luangwa

R. Rovuma

R. Kafue

R. Zambezi

R. Shire

*David Livingstone spent the last years of his life still exploring the
interior of the African continent.*

whether the Lualaba was actually the lower Congo River. (In fact, the Lualaba does flow into the Congo, not the Nile.)

By April 1873, as Livingstone and his men were exploring around Lake Bangweolo, he could barely continue his journey. He wrote, ". . . I could hardly walk, but tottered along nearly two hours, and then lay down, quite done." But a little later he continued. "Very unwilling to be carried, but on being pressed I allowed the men to help me along. . . ."[9] Unfortunately, Livingstone was too sick to travel much farther.

Later in April, the expedition stopped at the village of Chief Chitambo. Livingstone's men built a hut and a bed for him. Livingstone died there on May 1, 1873. The Africans who traveled with Livingstone decided to take his body back to the coast and return it to England. The Africans prepared the body, preserving it as well as possible. The internal organs were removed, and the heart was buried under a tree. Then the body was filled with salt and dried in the sun before being carried fifteen hundred miles eastward.

In England, Livingstone received a hero's funeral. In 1874, he was buried in London at Westminster Abbey, a church where some of Great Britain's most notable people are buried.

The Fame of Henry Stanley

Not only had Livingstone died a hero, but Stanley's fame was growing, too. He enjoyed every minute of it.

Westminster Abbey, where many English notables are buried, is the final resting place of David Livingstone.

On his way back from Africa, he had received a telegram from James Gordon Bennett: "You are now famous as Livingstone having discovered the discoverer. Accept my thanks, and whole world."[10]

Although Bennett was convinced Stanley's mission had succeeded, the British were not so sure. In fact, the Royal Geographical Society had already sent out another expedition to find Livingstone, when Stanley had run into them in Bagamoyo in 1872. He abruptly told them that they need not bother heading into the bush—Livingstone was fine. But the British were skeptical that an American—which Stanley claimed to be—could have beaten them to Livingstone. There was even talk in the British press that the letters and journals that Livingstone had given Stanley to take to England might be forgeries. But when Stanley finally returned to England and showed these papers to the government, there was no question that they were the real thing. Great Britain's Queen Victoria expressed her gratitude to Stanley by sending him a gift and a letter of thanks for his success in reaching Livingstone.

In 1873, Stanley published his book *How I Found Livingstone*. It became an enormous best-seller in both England and the United States. When Livingstone died that same year, Stanley was in West Africa, covering a war between Great Britain and the Ashanti nation. He later returned to London, where he served as one of the pall bearers at Livingstone's funeral.

Chapter 5

Stanley's Explorations

Stanley's relationship with Livingstone was very short, but it left a lasting impression on him. It also made Stanley extremely famous—something that was very important to him. Now he would have an opportunity to achieve even more.

Shortly after Livingstone's funeral, the editor of the London *Daily Telegraph* asked Stanley if he would like to follow in the great explorer's footsteps. The *Daily Telegraph* proposed to send Stanley back to Africa to explore Lake Victoria and determine whether it was the source of the Nile. He would also follow the Lualaba to discover whether it flowed into the Nile or the Congo. Not to be outdone by the *Daily Telegraph*, Livingstone's publisher, James Gordon Bennett, Jr., agreed to pay part of the cost of the expedition.

Stanley was very excited about the possibility of returning to Africa. He would be able not only to make some key discoveries as Livingstone had done, but could also achieve more recognition for himself. Finally, he could put to rest the doubts of all those who had questioned whether he had actually found Livingstone. "My tale of the discovery of Livingstone has been doubted," he wrote. "What I have already endured in that accursed Africa amounts to nothing, in men's estimation. Here, then, is an opportunity for me to prove my veracity [truthfulness], and the genuineness of my narrative!"[1]

In September 1874, Stanley returned to Zanzibar, where he had started his expedition to find Livingstone several years earlier. Zanzibar was no longer a center of the slave trade. After his meeting with Livingstone, Stanley had brought back to England the great explorer's descriptions of the massacre at Nyangwe by the Arab slave traders. This horrifying spectacle helped convince the British Parliament that it should do everything possible to eliminate the Arab slave trade. The British government had negotiated an agreement with the sultan (ruler) of Zanzibar to close the slave market— a negotiation reinforced by a British fleet anchored off the island. The sultan saw no choice but to close down slave trading on his island. As Stanley would discover, however, this did not necessarily mean that slavery had stopped on the African mainland.

Many of the Africans who had joined Stanley's expedition to locate Livingstone signed up again to accompany him to the interior. Stanley also brought men with him from England—hearty fishermen Frank and Edward Pocock, and Frederick Barker, a hotel clerk. To sail across Lake Victoria and along the Lualaba River, Stanley had brought a vessel that he called the *Lady Alice*, after a young woman named Alice Pike whom Stanley planned to marry after his return from Africa.

The Journey Begins

Stanley and his party left Zanzibar in early November, arrived in Bagamoyo, and soon afterward began the journey inland. Stanley was accompanied by more than three hundred men who served as guides and porters. They carried a large supply of trading goods to barter for food and to use to pay tribute to the tribes in the African interior.

During the early part of the trip, the heat was terrible. Two porters became sick. They were sent back to Bagamoyo. Others deserted. Stanley caught up with some of the deserters and clapped them into irons.

As the expedition headed north across the Merenga Mkali desert, they had to deal with a new problem—dehydration. Stanley and Frank Pocock had also contracted a fever, making travel even more difficult. As they reached the end of the desert, Africans met them "with gourds full of water for sale, which were eagerly bought up by . . . [us], who trudged on

Alice Pike was the woman Henry Stanley hoped to marry upon his return from his African expeditions. The marriage, however, never took place.

sore and distressed from heat and thirst. Many a gourd full of water was purchased for two yards of cloth on this day."[2]

During December, the brutal desert conditions were replaced by torrential rains. The expedition trekked through an area suffering from terrible famine. No food could be purchased to feed the men. Finally, near the end of the month, Stanley met a tribal chief named Masumami. The chief offered him some milk and a large ox in return for some trade goods. These helped reduce the hunger that had plagued his men. Nevertheless, many of them had already decided that they would go no farther. Fifty men planned to desert the expedition. Stanley discovered their plan before it could be carried out and had the ringleaders chained and whipped.

Though Stanley tried to control his guides and porters, he could do nothing to stop the rains. On January 4, 1875, he wrote that the walls of his tent

> enclosed a little lake, banked by boxes of stores, and ammunition. . . . [M]y bed was an island, with the water threatening to carry me off south with the flow. My shoes were become barks floating on a . . . tide. My guns lashed to the . . . tent pole were stock deep in water.[3]

That same month, Edward Pocock developed typhoid fever. This illness usually caused by contaminated water or milk. Pocock died on January 17. But Stanley refused to turn back. At one point, the expedition was attacked by the Waturu tribe. They

Traveling through the African wilderness could be dangerous and uncomfortable, especially for Europeans and Americans who were used to many luxuries.

refused to be bought off by tribute. While some of Stanley's men held off the attackers, the others built a wooden fence around their camp and set up wooden platforms where men with guns could stand and shoot at the enemy. Then Stanley brought all his men inside the stockade, where they spent the night. The next day, he went on the attack, sending out four groups of his men to burn the Waturu villages and steal their cattle. These detachments were successful, and the expedition proceeded northward with substantial food supplies.

Lake Victoria

In February, they finally reached Lake Victoria. They set up camp at the village of Kagehyi on its shores. There, they rested for a week and Stanley took stock of his men. "Over one-half of our force has . . . been lost by desertion and deaths," he wrote in one of his dispatches back to the newspapers:

> The dreadful scourge of the expedition has been dysentery [a disease that causes terrible diarrhea] and I can boast of but few men cured of it by medicine, though it was freely given. . . . A great drawback to their cure has been the necessity of moving on, whereas a few days' rest, in a country blessed with good water and food, would have restored many of them to health; but good water and good food could not be procured anywhere together except here.[4]

The *Lady Alice*, which had been carried in pieces along the trails, was now assembled on Lake Victoria. Leaving some of his party behind in a base camp at Kagehyi, Stanley spent the next two months exploring the lake with the rest of his men. There were many villages along the lake, but some of the tribes there were not interested in seeing white men encroach on their territory.

One group, called the Wavuma, approached the *Lady Alice* in canoes. They seemed interested in trading. But as the haggling began, the *Lady Alice* was soon surrounded by boatloads of warriors who came on board and began stealing trading goods. Stanley fired his gun, but the warriors were not frightened.

Stanley then fired at one man who had stolen some beads. Stanley's shot killed him. The other warriors now prepared to attack with their spears but Stanley rapidly killed several of them with his rifle. As they pushed off from the *Lady Alice* in their canoes, he made sure they would not return by firing at them with his huge elephant gun, which ripped into their boats.

As the *Lady Alice* sailed northward on the lake, Stanley entered the kingdom of Mtesa of Buganda (part of the modern nation of Uganda). Mtesa was a tall, impressive-looking man in his early thirties. He received Stanley at Usavara, the king's hunting camp on the lake. A few days later, Stanley joined the king to witness an impressive spectacle:

> Forty canoes with 30 men in each containing near 1200 men rowed races while [the king] and his 300 wives and upwards of 3000 spectators lined the shore to view the sport. I was called upon to exhibit my prowess in shooting. A young crocodile lay sleeping on a rock about 200 yards from shore, and rowing within 100 yards of it I had the good fortune . . . to shoot it.[5]

Mtesa had offered to give Stanley some warriors to defend his expedition as it moved westward away from Lake Victoria toward Lake Tanganyika. Most of these warriors never arrived, however, and Stanley continued his tour of Lake Victoria without them.

Stanley was successful in proving that Victoria was a single lake, not a series of small lakes, as some experts believed. In addition, Ripon Falls seemed to be the only major exit from the lake going northward.

Apparently, the explorer John Speke had been correct in believing that the Nile might originate in this area. However, Stanley still had to travel westward to the Lualaba to determine whether it flowed into the Nile.

The Journey Westward

As Stanley continued his journey westward around the lake on his way back to Kagehyi, his men again ran short of food. They tried to land on an island to trade with its people. As soon as the *Lady Alice* neared the shore, some warriors dragged it onto the beach. Barter goods of beads and cloth were given to the chief, who then retreated with his men. However, they took the oars of the boat, so Stanley could not leave.

After eating lunch, the warriors began to assemble, threatening to attack Stanley. He then ordered his men to push the *Lady Alice* into the water. They tore up some of the deck to use as oars and paddled away. When the warriors got in their canoes to follow him, Stanley used his elephant gun to kill some of them and sink their boats.

Eventually, he returned to Kagehyi in early May 1875. Gathering the rest of his men as well as the reinforcements that finally arrived from Mtesa, Stanley headed northward. He had hoped to explore the area due west of Lake Victoria. Once again, he encountered the island tribe that had given him so much trouble before. This time he lured them into a trap, killing and wounding a large number of them and putting their chief in chains. When word of this

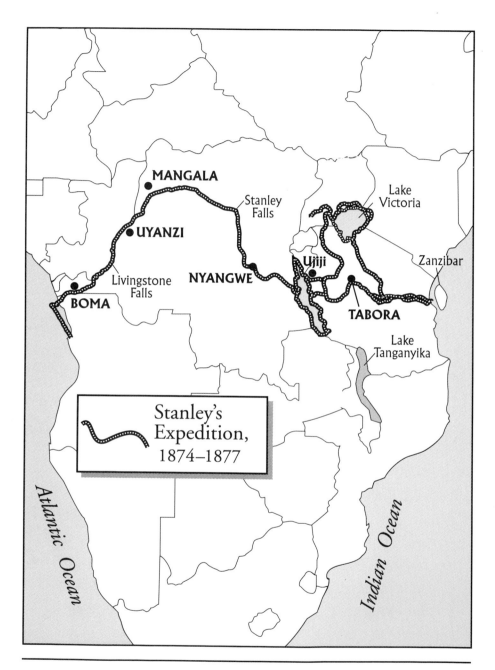

MANGALA

Stanley
Falls

Lake
Victoria

UYANZI

Zanzibar

Livingstone
Falls

NYANGWE

Ujiji

BOMA

TABORA

Lake
Tanganyika

Stanley's
Expedition,
1874–1877

Atlantic Ocean

Indian Ocean

Stanley's expedition was a difficult one, but he would eventually
find good routes across Africa that would help future trade.

reached England, Stanley was severely criticized. It seemed unnecessary to inflict more casualties on black Africans, who had only spears and shields to defend themselves:

> The hostile islanders had already been severely mauled in their first encounter with him, and all that the subsequent raid accomplished was to satisfy Stanley's need to "teach the natives a lesson" and enhance his growing . . . reputation as a ruthless conquistador to whom human life—especially black life—meant little.[6]

Stanley's efforts to move west from the shores of Lake Victoria were blocked by a hostile chief. This chief was so powerful that he even caused panic among the warriors of Mtesa. Stanley was eventually forced to head south, reaching Ujiji on the shores of Lake Tanganyika in May 1876. Stanley sailed around the lake, observing a slave caravan that he encountered along the way. A number of slaves had already died from starvation, including many children.

When he reached Nyangwe—the scene of the massacre witnessed by David Livingstone a few years earlier—Stanley sent a report to the newspapers. In it, he severely criticized the treatment of Africans by slave traders. But his distaste for the slave traders did not stop him from making a deal with one of them named Tippu Tib. Stanley needed the armed escort that Tippu Tib could provide to travel through an uncharted rain forest toward the Lualaba River. Otherwise, Stanley would have to turn back.

The journey through the rain forest proved extremely tough. The men had to cut their way through a dense jungle, sliding and scrambling along wet ground. Tippu Tib wanted to turn back, fearing the expedition would lose its way and his men would die. But Stanley persuaded him to continue. The expedition finally reached the Lualaba River in November.

Along the Lualaba

Stanley now divided his expedition. He sailed down the river in the *Lady Alice* with some of his men. Frank Pocock led the others along the shore. The vegetation was so thick that the two parties were quickly separated.

When Stanley sent out some of his men to find Pocock's party, they were attacked by African warriors. In December, Tippu Tib finally decided that his men had endured enough. He left the expedition. But Stanley would not turn back.

His men battled smallpox, attacks by people who shot them with poisoned arrows, and swirling rapids and treacherous waterfalls. Along a lengthy stretch of rapids—which Stanley would name Stanley Falls—the boats had to be carried overland. Stanley wrote:

> . . . we had fearful work, constructing camps by night along the line marked out during the day, cutting roads from above to below each fall, dragging our heavy canoes during the day, while the most active of the young men . . . repulsed the savages and foraged for food.[7]

Many of the tribes feared that Stanley's expedition was made up of slave traders who had come to carry them away.

Beyond Stanley Falls, the river began to grow wider but the expedition continued to encounter warriors who barred their way. At one point, Stanley counted fifty-four canoes coming toward him. One of them, which he described as a "monster," held "eighty paddlers, forty on a side, with paddles eight feet long. . . . On a platform near the bow were ten . . . fellows swaying their long spears ready."[8] But Stanley and his men drove them off with guns.

By mid-February, the expedition finally entered a more peaceful region. When they came upon a village where food was offered to them, Stanley used the opportunity to talk to the chief:

"What river is this, chief?" Stanley asked.

"The River," the chief replied.

"Has it no name?" Stanley asked.

"Yes, the Great River."

"I understand; but you have a name and I have a name, your village has a name. Have you no particular name for your river?"

"It is called Ikutu Ya Kongo."

The River of Congo![9]

The Lualaba had become the Congo. Stanley had solved one of the world's great geographical mysteries. The Lualaba was not, as Livingstone had believed, the source of the Nile. But the Lualaba and the Congo could be a good trade route through the African continent.

The Journey Ends

The expedition proceeded along the Congo River until it reached a lake that would become known as Stanley Pool. Beyond, there lay another long series of rapids and waterfalls, continuing for approximately one hundred fifty miles. The men made ropes of rattan, or palm, to tie onto the boats and hold them from the shore as they went downstream. Sometimes the ropes broke and the canoes were swept over the falls and destroyed. The men in one boat drowned when they lost control of their canoe in the powerful current.

Frank Pocock lost his life when his boat went over a waterfall. Stanley was very upset by Pocock's death. They had developed a close relationship, and Stanley relied on Pocock to help lead the expedition. Stanley wrote, ". . . I feel his loss as keenly as though he were my brother."[10] The porters and guides missed Pocock, too. Eventually, some of these men threatened a mutiny. They feared that, if they went any farther along this treacherous part of the river, all of them would die. Some actually left the expedition, but Stanley finally talked them into returning because they had no rifles or money to make their way back home.

By the end of July 1877, Stanley was nearing the west coast. With more rapids and waterfalls still left to cover, the expedition decided to leave the river and

Source Document

The rain, indeed, fell in such quantities that it required two men for each section to keep the boat sufficiently buoyant to ride the crest of the waves. The crew cried out that the boat was sinking—that, if the rain continued in such volume, nothing could save us. In reply, I only urged them to bale her out faster.[11]

Upon his return from his African expeditions, Henry Stanley wrote about his adventures in books that became best-sellers.

travel overland. After three days, the men were running short of food. Stanley sent some of his men ahead to a European trading settlement called Boma, hoping they could bring back supplies. Eventually, they returned and Stanley's expedition finished its trek across Africa. The entire journey had taken a thousand days.[12]

The journey along the Congo had proven extremely dangerous. Stanley admitted: "Had I the least suspicion that such a terrible series of Falls were before us, I should never have risked so many lives and such amount of money. . . ."[13] Although the trip had been very difficult, Stanley was convinced that the Congo had the potential to be a great avenue that could take Europeans into Africa. "The Congo is, and will be, the grand highway of commerce to West Central Africa," he wrote to the newspapers.[14]

Stanley, who had set out to solve a great geographical mystery, also hoped to follow in Livingstone's footsteps by trying to set up colonies in Africa. Stanley's belief in the future of the Congo would now transform the continent.

Leopold II and the Congo Free State

As Henry Stanley's articles about his expedition along the Congo appeared in the newspapers, they were eagerly read by people who had never been to Africa and wanted to know more about it. Among those most interested in Stanley's exploits was the tall, bearded monarch of a small country in western Europe. His name was Leopold II, king of the Belgians.

For many years, Leopold had been interested in creating colonies. As a prince, he had once spent days inside Spain's huge government archives in Seville. There, he absorbed all the facts and figures about the fabulous empire that had been established in the Western Hemisphere by the Spanish conquistadors. During the 1860s, Leopold's sister Carlota and her husband, Maximilian, had been sent to Mexico by

Napoleon III of France to establish a new empire. Carlota had come back to Europe a year before the Mexicans had overthrown and executed her husband. Though she had escaped with her life, Carlota had lost her mind because of her misfortunes. But his sister's tragedy did not stop Leopold from wanting to start his own empire.

Unfortunately, the Belgian government had no interest in establishing overseas colonies. Because the king was only a constitutional monarch with very little actual power, there seemed to be little he could do. Leopold, however, would soon find a way around this problem.

Leopold Turns to Africa

Leopold's father once described him as "subtle and sly," like a fox. "That is Leopold's way!" his father said.[1] Since Leopold could not irritate the Belgian government by openly advocating the founding of colonies, he decided to go about it in a more indirect way. He was determined to become a great colonial monarch like his cousin, England's Queen Victoria, who already ruled a large empire.

In 1876, while Henry Stanley was still struggling through Africa, Leopold was holding what he called a Geographical Conference in Brussels, the capital of Belgium. He had invited famous explorers and other notables, such as the head of Great Britain's Anti-Slavery Society, to meet at his offices in the Royal Palace. There, they discussed the concept of

Source Document

After 1870, [Great Britain's] manufacturing and trading supremacy was greatly impaired: other nations, especially Germany, the United States, and Belgium, advanced with great rapidity, and while they have not crushed or even stayed the increase of our external trade, their competition made it more and more difficult to dispose of the full surplus of our manufactures at a profit. The encroachments made by these nations upon our old markets, even in our own possessions, made it most urgent that we should take energetic means to secure new markets. These new markets had to lie in hitherto undeveloped countries, chiefly in the tropics, where vast populations lived capable of growing economic needs which our manufacturers and merchants could supply.[2]

In 1902, British writer John Hobson described the economic reasons behind European imperialism in such places as Africa.

establishing bases along the Congo River that would be charged with doing scientific research, teaching new skills to the Africans, providing them with medical care, and eliminating slavery. The conference also decided to create the International African Association, with Leopold as its chairman. On the surface, the king's efforts looked innocent enough— he simply wanted to help the people in Africa. But in reality, he was taking the first step toward developing a vast empire.

Leopold realized, however, that he could not travel to the Congo and embark on the process of empire building himself. He needed someone who knew the territory, someone with the determination to carve out a large colony no matter what the dangers. He needed Henry Stanley.

As Stanley was returning to England after his African expedition, Leopold sent representatives to offer the explorer a position with the International African Association. Stanley turned it down. He wanted to reach London, where a hero's welcome awaited him. He also believed that England was the logical choice to step in and assert control over the Congo River. He believed only the British could prevent a conflict from breaking out as European merchants arrived and confronted the African tribes who lived there.

Though the English acclaimed Stanley as a great explorer, the British government had no interest in stepping into central Africa. Some officials were

King Leopold II, hoping to build a huge empire for himself, tried to hire Henry Stanley to help.

suspicious of Stanley because of reports that he had mistreated his African porters, burned villages, and taken revenge on poorly armed warriors along Lake Victoria. Meanwhile, Leopold continued to urge Stanley to reconsider and join the association.

When Stanley realized that the British government had no intention of following his recommendations in Africa, he finally decided to meet with Leopold in 1878. Because Stanley was on a speaking tour for his new book about the expedition across the African continent, he was in no hurry to take on any new responsibilities. But Leopold and his key officials kept up the pressure. Stanley finally accepted an offer to return to Africa.

Back to Africa

In February 1879, Stanley left for the African continent. He had agreed to head an expedition that would be financed by an international investment group. Although Leopold was the leader of the group, this information was kept largely secret.

Stanley traveled to Zanzibar, where he hired some men for his expedition. He then headed back to the Suez Canal, through the Mediterranean Sea, toward the west coast of Africa. He eventually arrived at Boma. His task was to build a roadway along the Congo, bypassing the treacherous rapids, until he had reached Stanley Pool. There, steamboats, which had been carried in pieces along the road, would be assembled, and the men would sail along the thousand-mile course of the river as it flowed to Stanley Falls. Along the way, a series of stations would be built. Each station would represent the International Association of the Congo, a new organization established under Leopold's direction, supposedly to improve the lives of the people in Africa.

Its true purpose, however, was far different. Stanley was expected to build trading posts, where he would acquire ivory from the African tribes in the area. The demand for ivory in Europe was huge—for everything from piano keys and small statues to combs and false teeth. Leopold wanted to exploit this demand, build an empire for himself in Africa, and at the same time, acquire vast riches.

The Work Begins

After arriving at Boma, Stanley pushed inland. He built his first station, Vivi, at the rapids. Then his men began the difficult task of building a road around the long stretch of rapids on the way to Stanley Pool. In stifling heat, they had to hack through undergrowth and dig their way through huge stretches of solid rock so they could lay the roadway. It was during this ordeal that Stanley received the name from the African workers that "he was to prize for the rest of his life: Bula Matari—Smasher of Rocks."[3]

The work was backbreaking and incredibly slow. By February 1881, he had established only a second station, at Isangila, fifty miles from Vivi. During the first year of the expedition, Stanley had lost twenty-eight men to disease and other causes, including being eaten by a crocodile.[4]

Stanley drove everyone, including himself, very harshly. Speaking of the Africans who labored under him, Stanley wrote: "It takes some time to drill and discipline a body of raw negroes. . . . Punishment must be in two forms only—the stick or whip—and irons. . . ."[5] While Stanley did not hesitate to punish the African workers physically, he also had very little tolerance for Europeans who had come along on the expedition but could not deal with the rigors of Africa. He described many of them as "always weak and ailing in health, who have to be carried about and instructed like little children. . . ."[6]

Although Stanley liked to believe that he was far too tough for any illness to slow him down, he almost died of malaria. A "severe fever" gripped him in June 1881. Gravely ill, he called everyone together and "I gave my farewell—and my last instructions; then, while conversing the last agony came and I was unconscious again. . . ." He awoke two days later and recovered.[7]

Stanley Faces Competition

Eventually, Stanley reached Stanley Pool, only to find that a fort had already been built there by a French expedition led by a naval officer named Pierre Savorgnan de Brazza. Brazza had signed a treaty with a chief in the area. In it, Brazza established French interests on the north side of Stanley Pool. By the time

Stanley finally arrived, the French had instructed all the chiefs not to sell any food to Stanley's party.

Stanley went to the south side of the pool, where he had to deal with a powerful chief named Ngaliema. At first, the chief tried to intimidate Stanley and marched to his camp with a group of armed warriors. Unknown to Ngaliema, Stanley realized he was coming and had hidden his own men in the underbrush. As the chief arrived with his warriors, Stanley pretended to be unconcerned in the presence of so many men. Suddenly, Ngaliema spied a large gong that Stanley had hung nearby. When the chief asked what it was, Stanley told him: "The slightest sound of that would fill this empty camp with hundreds of angry warriors; they would drop from above, they would spring up from the ground, from the forest about, from everywhere." Ngaliema did not believe him. He said it was a story for old women. So Stanley struck the gong. His men magically appeared, yelling loudly to frighten Ngaliema's soldiers. Stanley remembered, "The painted warriors became panic-stricken; they flung their guns . . . away, forgot their chief, and all thoughts of loyalty, and fled. . . ." Although Ngaliema remained behind, he, too, was frightened. Stanley vowed to protect him from any harm.[8] It would take more confrontations as well as lengthy negotiations before Ngaliema finally agreed to provide ivory in return for trade goods, despite the treaty with Brazza.

At Stanley Pool, Stanley established a trading post, which he called Leopoldville, after the Belgian king. Then he proceeded upriver in his steamboat to set up more stations. Unfortunately, he developed a severe fever once again and was brought back to Leopoldville, extremely sick. In July 1882, he returned to Europe.

The Expedition Continues

Stanley spent very little time recovering his health. Leopold persuaded him to return to Africa near the end of the year. No one else, the king was convinced, could ensure the success of his new venture along the Congo. When Stanley came back to the trading stations on the river, he found that the commanders left in charge of them had failed to maintain peaceful relations with the African tribes. So Stanley set about repairing the damage.

He was supported by a formidable military force, including "about a hundred white men, six hundred blacks, eight steamers . . . four machine-guns, a thousand quick-firing [repeating] rifles . . . over two million cartridges, etc."[9] Nothing like this had ever been seen along the river. It must have impressed the local tribes.

Stanley had been instructed by King Leopold to sign treaties with as many chiefs as possible. The king hoped the chiefs would sign over all their rights to the territories under their control. This included any roads or rivers, and any rights to forests, minerals, or animals. The treaties would also contain an agreement to provide any men necessary to improve the area. As historian Adam Hochschild wrote, "many chiefs had no idea what they were signing."[10] They were tricked by Stanley and by King Leopold. In return for giving up their lands, the chiefs received a few pieces of cloth and a handful of other items. But Stanley had given Leopold control of the Congo River basin, keeping the French or any other power from claiming it first.

In 1884, Stanley returned to Europe. In the meantime, King Leopold had been winning recognition for his new venture from other nations. Late in 1883, Leopold had sent one of his

An artist depicted Stanley and the members of his expedition as they cut their way through the "Dark Continent," as Africa was called.

representatives, an American named Henry Sanford, to Washington, D.C., to convince United States President Chester Alan Arthur to recognize the association's claims in Africa. Sanford claimed that the king was simply trying to repeat the effort made by the United States years earlier in Liberia, which was founded in 1821 as a safe haven for freed African-American slaves. Leopold also assured President Arthur that the Congo would be a free-trade area for United States companies and that every effort would be made to eliminate slavery in the area.

On April 22, 1884, the United States became the first country to recognize Leopold's new domain. France made a similar decision, because the Belgian king made the French government a very attractive offer. Leopold guaranteed that, if he should pull out of the area for lack of funds, it would be offered to France. This would prevent Great Britain from moving into the area, which the French feared might happen. Finally, Leopold convinced German Chancellor Otto von Bismark to support his claims by offering Germany free trade in the area. Bismark was also happier to have Belgium in control of Africa than the more powerful French or British.

In 1884, Bismark hosted a conference in Berlin. It included delegates from the major nations in Europe. The focus of their interest was Africa, which had begun to receive more attention following the explorations of David Livingstone and Henry Stanley. Stanley himself was also present at the meeting. As a

Otto von Bismark, the chancellor of Germany, helped start the Scramble for Africa with his participation in the Berlin Conference.

result of the Berlin Conference, a large free-trade zone was established in central Africa. The Congo, controlled by Leopold, became part of this trading zone. Shortly after the conference ended, the king announced that the area he was developing in Africa would now be known as the Congo Free State.

The Congo Free State

Although the delegates at the Berlin Conference might have believed that free trade had been established in the Congo, Leopold had no intention of allowing it. Instead, he planned to use the area to make himself and his partners rich. Part of the region was directly developed by Leopold, but he lacked the money to develop all of it. The enormous territory stretched for nine hundred thousand square miles. What Leopold could not develop himself, he leased to private companies. In return, he received more than half the profits that they made.

Companies from other nations were kept out of the so-called free state. Meanwhile, Leopold's agents used every means available to take as much ivory as possible from the countryside. Sometimes they would shoot elephants themselves. More frequently, they relied on African hunters to bring in their loads of ivory for sale. They also issued stern warnings that they were the only ones to whom Africans could sell their ivory. In return for the ivory tusks, the Africans were given only meager amounts of trade goods. European agents were awarded extra commissions for getting the ivory at the lowest possible prices. Then it was sold at huge profits in Europe.

Although slavery was supposedly outlawed in the Congo Free State, the Africans were treated no better than slaves. Porters were needed to carry supplies over any area where river travel was impossible. Often they were chained together, receiving little to eat and even less in pay. If they tried to leave, they were brought back and often lashed by an overseer who used a chicotte, a special sharp-edged whip made of sun-dried hippopotamus hide. Many men died after receiving repeated lashings from the chicotte. Others

The European demand for ivory put native Africans in dangerous situations that were often very unfair.

collapsed in the terrible African heat as they tried to carry heavy loads of ivory or other supplies along the roadways.

To keep control over the Congo, Leopold established a police force known as the Force Publique. Because they were very poorly paid, black soldiers had to be drafted into the force. There, they were commanded by white officers, who used the chicotte regularly to keep them in line. Whites in the Congo rationalized their treatment of the Africans by claiming that they were an inferior, lazy race of people who deserved whatever punishment they received. Earlier, Southern planters in the United States had used the same arguments to justify slavery.

The plight of the Africans grew even worse during the 1890s as the demand for rubber grew in Europe. Rubber was used for bicycle tires, and later automobile tires, as well as insulation for telephone wires and tubing for machinery. In the Congo, rubber could be found in vines that grew high in the treetops. The vines were tapped and the liquid rubber flowed out to be collected in pots and dried. Collecting rubber could be dangerous work. Men were required to climb high into the trees to tap the rubber after the supply had already been tapped from the vines near the ground.

This was not the type of work that most native Africans would readily volunteer to do, especially for the low wages the Europeans were likely to pay them. Yet the profits were huge—sometimes more than 700 percent—if agents could collect a large supply of

Source Document

A slight clinking behind me made me turn my head. Six black men advanced in a file, toiling up the path. They walked erect and slow, balancing small baskets full of earth on their heads, and the clink kept time with their footsteps. Black rags were wound round their loins, and the short ends waggled to and fro like tails. I could see every rib, the joints of their limbs were like knots in a rope; each had an iron collar on his neck, and all were connected together with a chain whose bights swung between them, rhythmically clinking.[11]

Writer Joseph Conrad's 1902 work, Heart of Darkness, *described the terrible way Europeans treated native Africans after planting colonies on the continent.*

rubber and ship it to Europe.[12] To force African men to collect rubber, King Leopold's agents began taking women and children as hostages. They were held in stockades and given very little to eat until the men of the village returned with what the Europeans deemed an acceptable amount of rubber. Then the women and children were released, and the men were paid a little cloth and a few beads for risking their lives. Any African man who did not collect his quota of rubber would be whipped with the chicotte. Any village that did not agree to participate in the rubber collecting scheme risked being massacred by European Congo officials.

King Leopold II claimed that he had established the Congo Free State to benefit the Africans who lived there. The reality was far different.

Chapter 7

The Scramble for Africa

In 1881, as Henry Stanley and Pierre de Brazza led their expeditions along the Congo River in a race to take control of the area, they began a new stage in European expansion. It would later be known as the Scramble for Africa.[1]

The Scramble for African Colonies

The "scramble" was an effort by European nations to develop large colonial empires on the African continent. For centuries, these countries had maintained trading stations along the African coast. During the nineteenth century, the development of the steamboat helped explorers like Stanley transport men and supplies up the Congo into the African interior. Superior weapons like the machine gun and the repeating rifle, which fired multiple shots without reloading, also meant that Stanley and others like him could overcome the resistance of the native Africans, who usually fought with spears and bows and arrows or, at best, single-shot rifles.

But it was not simply advanced technology that produced these new colonies. It was the power of imperialism—a desire among Europeans to force their civilization and their economic control on the African continent. Imperialism arose, in part, because of an intense nationalism among nations such as France, Germany, and Great Britain. Colonies symbolized national power and national pride. Each of these countries saw the others as rivals. Each wanted to plant its own flag on a large piece of Africa before any other country claimed it. Although Leopold was operating for himself, not the Belgian government, he, too, developed a flag for the Congo Free State—blue with a gold star.

There were other strong motives for imperialism. Colonies would open up new markets for goods manufactured in Europe. Factory owners believed they could sell items such as clothing, agricultural equipment, and building supplies to the Africans. This would not only make European factories more prosperous, but also employ more workers. That would mean more money for everyone. Africa also represented a potentially lucrative area for investment. Huge profits could be made in the ivory and rubber that were being harvested in the Congo Free State, or from the gold and diamond mines that had been discovered in South Africa. The cost of labor on the continent was cheap because European companies, operating with the blessing of their governments, paid African workers very low wages.

Missionaries also came to Africa during the scramble, hoping to bring Christianity and Western education to the Dark Continent, as Europeans often called Africa because of its unfamiliar jungles, deserts, and people. They felt it was the obligation of the white race to "uplift" Africans. But there was frequently little they could do to prevent the continent or its people from being exploited by any country with the spirit of adventure and greed necessary to march into the interior and take control.

Establishing Colonies

By the last quarter of the nineteenth century, European nations were already struggling for control in many parts of Africa. In western Africa, for example, France and Great Britain were trying to establish spheres of influence along the Niger and Senegal rivers. A major prize was palm oil—a raw material used to lubricate machinery in factories and a basic ingredient in soap. Each nation was afraid that the other might establish a monopoly by achieving dominance over the African tribes in the area. They led expeditions into the interior, established military posts, and signed agreements with tribal chiefs to get the upper hand in the palm oil trade. Finally, Great Britain and France had to agree to share control in the area. Their spheres of influence were recognized by the Berlin Conference in 1885. Eventually, Great Britain established a colony in Nigeria, along with other colonies in Sierra Leone and the Gold Coast. French colonies included Senegal as well as Dahomey and the Ivory Coast. Meanwhile, Pierre de Brazza's efforts had helped France establish a colony along the Congo River, and Brazzaville became the capital of French Equatorial Africa.

From the time of the Berlin Conference, European colonial expansion intensified. Germany had already acquired territory in southwest Africa. On the east coast of Africa, the power of the sultan of Zanzibar had declined. Germany saw an opportunity to acquire a huge territory on the mainland. Led by an explorer named Carl Peters, Germany was busy creating a large colony in east Africa. However, the German presence seemed to threaten Great Britain's trading interests and its support for the sultan. Eventually, in 1886, Great Britain and Germany decided to separate the area into spheres of influence. Germany would control an area south of Mombasa and inland to Lake Victoria. British interests would lie north of this line. The sultan would still maintain his presence along the coast.

North Africa: Stanley Returns

Meanwhile, in North Africa, the power of European imperialism was also growing stronger. Earlier in the nineteenth century, France had taken control of

AFRICA

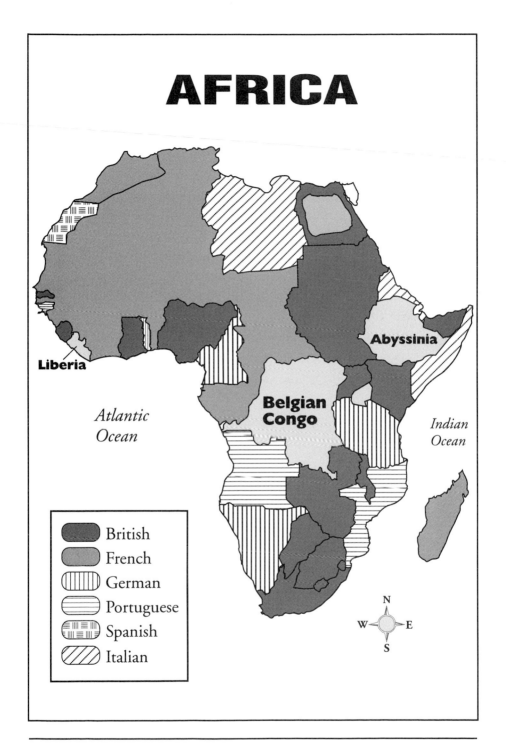

Liberia

Atlantic
Ocean

Abyssinia

Belgian
Congo

Indian
Ocean

Legend:
- British
- French
- German
- Portuguese
- Spanish
- Italian

N
W — E
S

*By the early years of the twentieth century, almost every European
power had taken a slice of Africa as a colony.*

Algeria, which had been part of the Turkish Empire. In 1881, the French Army invaded Tunis. The French came supposedly to help the bey (Turkish governor) of Tunis deal with some rebellious tribesmen who were attacking Algeria. Once the invasion was successful and the rebellion put down, the French remained in control of Tunis.

In Egypt, France and Great Britain had imposed a similar arrangement. They reduced the khedive (head of state) to a figurehead because he had been bankrupting the country, threatening the investments of French and British banks. Meanwhile, a much larger problem had arisen south, in the Sudan, which was nominally under Egyptian control. A Muslim leader called the Mahdi had begun a revolt that had swept across the desert. By 1883, he held most of the Sudan. The khedive sent British General Charles Gordon south to rescue the remaining Egyptian garrisons in the Sudan. Instead, Gordon was trapped by the Mahdi's forces in Khartoum, the capital, with all of his men. In January 1885, Khartoum fell and Gordon was killed before a British relief force could reach him.

Farther south, in Sudan's Equatoria Province, Governor Emin Bey was trying to hold off the Mahdi's forces with an army of four thousand Sudanese troops. In 1886, he succeeded in sending out a letter to the British government, saying that he would continue to defend his territory until help could arrive. The British government was reluctant at first to send a costly and dangerous expedition to help him. After all, Emin was

This illustration depicts the murder of General Gordon at Khartoum.

a German. Perhaps his own government should undertake the effort to relieve him. In England, however, there was growing public opinion that something should be done to rescue a man as brave as Emin. The most experienced man for the job was the same one who had rescued David Livingstone fifteen years earlier—Henry Stanley.

Stanley to the Rescue

After money had been raised for his expedition, Stanley collected arms and ammunition to transport to Emin's troops. Many Englishmen also wanted to join the popular rescue effort. Stanley selected several of them, including Lieutenant Grant Stairs, Captain Robert Nelson, army surgeon Thomas Parke, and Mounteney Jephson, who had made financial contributions to the expedition. In early 1887, Stanley arrived in Zanzibar and met with Tippu Tib, who was supposed to supply him with porters. He also sent a letter to Emin, saying he would meet him on Lake Albert, south of Equatoria.

Stanley might have decided to head inland from the east coast, past Lake Victoria to Lake Albert. This would have appealed to English merchants, who wanted to expand Great Britain's sphere of influence in East Africa. Instead, he chose to travel to the west coast of Africa, sail up the Congo, and then head north to Yambuya and follow the Aruwimi River to Lake Albert. Stanley seemed to believe that this was a better route. It also appealed to King Leopold, for whom Stanley still worked. Leopold wanted to expand the Congo Free State northward. Stanley could explore the area between its current boundaries and Equatoria. In addition, Leopold was prepared to offer Emin a position as governor of this territory, which would become part of the Congo Free State.

The Expedition Begins

By March 1887, Stanley and his men were already on the Congo. The journey, however, was extremely difficult. By the time they reached Leopoldville at Stanley Pool, some of Stanley's men had died. Others were sick, and some of the porters had deserted. Although Leopold had promised steamboats to ferry the men farther up the river, these were in a state of disrepair. Stanley almost forcibly had to take steamboats from some of the missionaries in the area. As the expedition proceeded upstream, there were reports that Stanley was very harsh in criticizing the men he had brought from England. He also had little respect for the porters he had picked up in Zanzibar. "Their heads were uncommonly empty," he wrote.[2] At Yambuya, Stanley left a small force to await supplies and a larger group of porters that had been promised by Tippu Tib. In June, he left with the rest of his men through the dense Ituri rain forest.

Stanley described the rain forest as a "wilderness of creeks, mud, thick scum-faced quagmires green with duckweed into which we sank knee-deep, and the stench . . . was most sickening."[3] While part of his

Henry Stanley, because of his experience traveling in the African interior, was sent to rescue Emin.

force could proceed on the Aruwimi, the rest had to cut a trail along the river. As his men came upon a village, they had to watch where they walked. Hidden on the ground were "poisoned skewers," which could penetrate even the boots of the white soldiers.

The men who traveled on the river had to battle rapids and other dangers. As they tried to brace themselves while going over one set of rapids, they grasped overhanging branches, "but at the first clutch there issued . . . an army of fierce spiteful wasps, which settled on our faces, hands, and bodies, every vulnerable spot, and stung us with the venom of fiends."[4] Native Africans attacked Stanley's expedition with poisoned arrows. Historian John Bierman wrote that the tribesmen feared a return of the Arab slave traders: "But as Stanley's column advanced, taking whatever food they could find if barter was impossible, seizing women and children as guides and hostages, sometimes burning deserted villages, they created hostility on their own account."[5]

As Stanley's expedition dealt with the severe conditions of the rain forest, he began to wonder if they would ever reach their goal of rescuing Emin.[6] Eventually, they met an Arab slave-trading party that sold them some food. Stanley also left many of his sick and wounded in the care of the Arabs and pushed on northward. By early October, many of his men were weakened by lack of food. Fifty of the weakest men were left behind under Captain Nelson with a small food supply while Stanley set out to find another slave party that was supposed to be nearby. By the time he found their camp and convinced them to send food back to his other men, most of those men had deserted or died. Mounteney Jephson had gone back to pick them up, but by the time he returned to the slavers' camp, Stanley had already departed, leaving behind another group that had become too sick to travel.

Eventually, Jephson caught up with Stanley, who had finally reached an area where more food was available. The expedition was forced to battle African tribal warriors who blocked their way northward. They did not reach Lake Albert until the middle of December 1887.

Finding Emin

When Stanley finally camped at a village on Lake Albert, he discovered that there had been no communication from Emin. Because he had been forced to leave his boat behind earlier, Stanley could not sail across the lake to find Emin and his soldiers. Therefore, he decided to retreat and establish a strong base. Out of the wilderness, Stanley and his men carved Fort Bodo. They planted crops, started collecting food, and sent out an expedition under Lieutenant Stairs to collect the boat as well as the sick and wounded who had been left behind. In April, Stanley returned to Lake Albert. There, he found a message from Emin. It said Emin was prepared to come across the lake for a meeting.

When the two leaders finally met, Stanley realized that his force was in far worse condition than Emin's. By rescuing him, Stanley had hoped not only to save Emin from being massacred by the Mahdi, but also to win glory and acclaim for himself, just as he had done in finding Livingstone. But Emin explained that he had no need to be rescued and did not want to leave Equatoria. His soldiers had driven back the Mahdi's forces, and his territory seemed more secure. He also had no interest in making a deal with King Leopold to become an employee of the Congo Free State. Although Stanley tried to urge Emin to change his mind, Emin insisted that he was not ready to leave.

Apparently, the entire expedition had been a waste of time. It had cost many lives and left Stanley looking like a fool. But it was not quite over. Stanley left Jephson with Emin and returned to Fort Bodo. He rejoined Captain Nelson, who had been left in charge of the garrison. A short time later, Stanley was off again. This time, he took a party of men with him to find the rearguard that was supposed to be marching northward with supplies and the porters promised by Tippu Tib. Stanley retraced his steps. He finally found what was left of the rear column at Banalya on the Aruwimi River. The commander of this detachment had been murdered by one of the porters, who then began to loot the supplies. Other men had also been killed during the looting. After arriving at Banalya, Stanley gathered up the remnants of his force and returned to Fort Bodo before the end of 1888.

Rescuing Emin

In the meantime, there had been no further word from Emin. Still, Stanley decided to go back to Lake Albert and make one more attempt at "rescuing" him. While Stanley had been away at Banalya, conditions in Equatoria had deteriorated. The Mahdi's forces had attacked again. Emin and Jephson had been held hostage for a while by the governor's own rebellious soldiers. Although they had been freed from captivity, Emin's position in Equatoria seemed dangerous. Nevertheless, when he met with Stanley, Emin was hesitant to leave Equatoria. Finally, Stanley threatened to abandon him. Emin decided to go.

The combined expedition headed southeast, skirting Lake Victoria. They rested for several weeks at an English mission station under the direction of the Reverend Alexander Mackay. Since coming to the area in 1877, Mackay had managed to convert a number of Africans to Christianity. The expedition then continued to Mpwapwa, where it was met by German soldiers who were patrolling Germany's sphere of influence in East Africa. Eventually, Stanley and Emin arrived at Bagamoyo in December 1889. "We are at home!" Stanley said. "Yes, thank God," Emin replied.[7]

Emin decided not to return to England with Stanley. Instead, he remained in Africa and worked for the German foreign service, trying to enlarge Germany's colonial territories. Stanley went back to England. He was welcomed as a hero. He became

Henry Stanley, as he looked in his later years.

engaged to a woman named Dorothy Tennant, with whom he had been involved in an on-again, off-again relationship. They were married at Westminster Abbey in July 1890.

Stanley also wrote another best-seller—this one based on his efforts to "rescue" Emin—and he went on a lecture tour of the United States, accompanied by his wife. He never led another African expedition. He decided instead to enter politics. He won a seat in the British Parliament, which he held from 1895 to 1900. Stanley died in 1904.

Chapter 8

The Legacy of Stanley and Livingstone

Both David Livingstone and Henry Morton Stanley were men determined to achieve their goals. In pursuit of them, they started the Scramble for Africa. Livingstone was born in poverty, yet he had the strength to overcome his background—a quality that served him well as he dealt with the hardships of exploring the African wilderness. Why did he choose to go to Africa? At first, he went there to convert the people to Christianity. Many missionaries, like Livingstone, believed strongly that Christianity would uplift the African people and enable them to enjoy more satisfying spiritual lives. Soon after arriving in Africa, Livingstone realized that the continent suffered from the cruel injustices of slavery. One of the ways that African tribes acquired wealth was to sell other Africans, whom they defeated in battle, to

European and Muslim slave traders. Livingstone dedicated much of his life to trying to eliminate slavery. But he was practical enough to realize that slavery could not be removed unless he brought other benefits to the continent—economic improvements that involved bringing European merchants to Africa to trade with the tribes and start colonies there. All along, Livingstone was also driven by his own ambition to be a great explorer—even if it meant sacrificing the lives of the men who traveled with him.

Stanley was driven by similar motives. Born an illegitimate child, he was determined to achieve respectability and international fame. He achieved both of these things by finding Livingstone and writing a best-seller about it, but he did not stop there. He led an expedition across the African continent. Then he helped establish the Congo Free State—which quickly became one of Africa's most repressive regimes. Although he was bold and courageous—the hallmarks of a highly successful explorer—Stanley regarded Africans as his inferiors. He could be extremely cruel to the men who served with him, whether they were white or black.

Together, Stanley and Livingstone helped bring imperialism to Africa. Although Livingstone would not live long enough to see colonies established that would bring European commerce to every part of the African interior, Stanley would play a key role in turning Livingstone's dream into reality.

Source Document

. . . Whereas denial of the franchise to Africans on the basis of race or sex has been one of the principal instruments of colonial policy by imperialists and their agents, thus making it feasible for a few white settlers to lord it over millions of indigenous Africans. . . . Be it resolved and it is hereby resolved by; the All-African People's Conference meeting in Accra 5th to 13th December, 1958, and comprising over 300 delegates representing over 200 million Africans from all parts of Africa . . . the All-African People's Conference vehemently condemns colonialism and imperialism in whatever shape or form these evils are perpetuated. . . .[1]

During the middle of the twentieth century, many African natives banded together to try to win back power from the Europeans who still administered the governments of many African colonies.

But empire building involves both winners and losers. While European colonists often benefited from the new empires that stretched across Africa, the Africans themselves were frequently exploited. Europeans often occupied the best land and forced the Africans to work for them. What few African farmers remained were often forced to give up

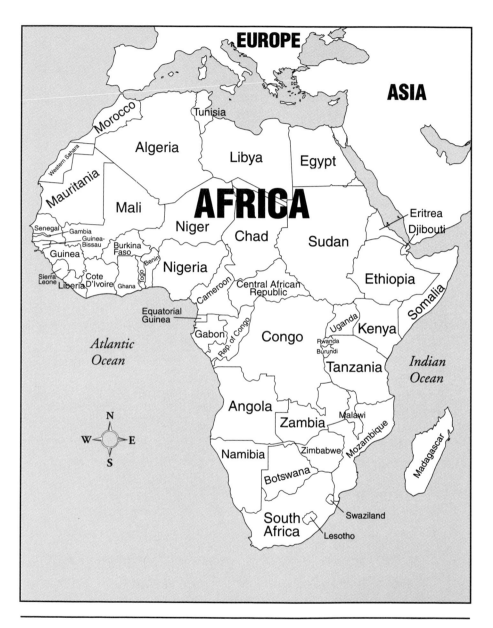

The continent of Africa today contains many independent nations, no longer part of European empires. The legacy of the Scramble for Africa, however, can still be seen in the relatively poor conditions faced by many of the native African people.

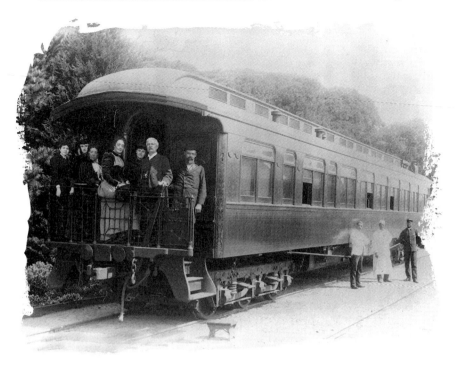

Stanley and some of his friends take a train tour in Africa in 1891

growing food crops in favor of crops, such as coffee, that could be exported to Europe at a profit. As a result, famine became more common in Africa.

As the European countries carved out colonies in Africa, they also disregarded traditional tribal boundaries. Consequently, tribes that had long been in conflict with each other found themselves forced to live together in the same colony.

The colonial administrators tried to bring some of the advantages of European civilization to the Africans. Railroads were built across the continent.

Urban trading centers were developed with modern buildings. Some government officials believed they had a responsibility to take up the "white man's burden"—to improve conditions among the African people by bringing them the supposedly superior civilization of white Europeans. A small number of Africans were educated at schools, usually run by Christian missionaries, and a few went to Europe to attend college. However, these benefits came only with the sacrifice of tribal lands, customs, and traditions.

After World War II, it was these educated Africans who began to press the European powers to give their colonies independence. Around 1960, independence began to be achieved by most African nations after years of struggle against the European colonial governments. In many cases, the Africans who ran the new governments imposed dictatorships on their countries. Meanwhile, most of the people remained poor farmers. The Europeans had never set up any industries in their colonies or trained the Africans to work in manufacturing. Despite claims of bringing European civilization, the benefits of European wealth never really reached the native people of Africa. In addition, the African nations were regularly being torn apart by intense conflict among rival tribes who had been forced by the Europeans to live together. All of these problems—the dark side of the legacy of Stanley and Livingstone—continue to plague the African continent today.

1813—David Livingstone is born in Blantyre, Scotland.

1833—Great Britain abolishes slavery in its empire.

1837—Victoria becomes queen of England.

1840—Livingstone completes medical school.

1841—Livingstone arrives in Africa; Henry Stanley is born in Wales as John Rowlands.

1843—Livingstone establishes a new mission in Mabotsa.

1845—Livingstone marries Mary Moffat.

1849—Livingstone becomes the first European to reach Lake Ngami.

1853 –1856—Livingstone travels across the African continent.

1855—Livingstone names Victoria Falls.

1858 –1859—Livingstone explores the Zambesi River and reaches Lake Nyasa.

1858—Explorers Richard Burton and John Speke reach Lake Tanganyika.

1859 –1863—Livingstone explores the Zambesi and Shire rivers.

1859—Stanley arrives in New Orleans, Louisiana.

1861—Civil War begins in the United States.

1862—Stanley fights at Battle of Shiloh.

1865—Civil War ends.

1866 –1871—Livingstone searches for the source of the Nile River.

1868—Stanley covers the war in Abyssinia.

1871—Stanley finds Livingstone.

1871 –1873—Livingstone continues his search for the source of the Nile.

1873—Livingstone dies.

1874 –1877—Stanley leads an expedition across the African continent.

1879 –1884—Stanley and Leopold II of Belgium establish the Congo Free State.

1885—Berlin Conference discusses future of Africa; Khartoum in the Sudan falls to the forces of the Mahdi.

1887 –1889—Stanley leads an expedition to rescue Emin Bey in the Sudan.

1890—Stanley marries Dorothy Tennant.

1895 –1900—Stanley serves in Parliament.

1904—Stanley dies.

Chapter Notes

Chapter 1.   "Dr. Livingstone, I Presume?"

1. Henry M. Stanley, *How I Found Livingstone* (New York: Charles Scribner's Sons, 1872), p. xvii.

2. Dr. James Macnair, ed., *Livingstone's Travels* (New York: Macmillan, 1954), p. 342.

3. Stanley, p. 135.

4. Ibid., p. 161.

5. Ibid., p. 412.

6. H. M. Stanley, "Stanley Finds Livingstone, 10 November 1871," *Eyewitness to History*, ed. John Carey (New York: Avon Books, 1987), p. 388.

Chapter 2. Dr. Livingstone in Africa

1. Project Gutenberg, "Missionary Travels in South Africa," *Project Gutenberg Etexts*, 1971–1999, <ftp://sunsite.unc.edu/pub/docs/books/gutenberg/etext97/mtrav10.txt> (October 22, 1999).

2. Tim Jeal, *Livingstone* (New York: G. P. Putnam's, 1973), pp. 38–39.

3. Ibid., p. 78.

4. Dr. James I. Macnair, ed., *Livingstone's Travels* (New York: Macmillan, 1954), pp. 23–24.

5. I. Schapera, ed., *Livingstone's Missionary Correspondence, 1841–1856* (Berkeley: University of California Press, 1961), p. 241.

6. Macnair, p. 73.

7. Schapera, p. 263.

8. Macnair, p. 151.

9. Ibid., p. 173.

10. David Livingstone, "Discovering Victoria Falls. Africa, 1856," *The Mammoth Book of Eyewitness History*, ed. Jon E. Lewis (New York: Carroll & Graf Publishers, Inc., 1998), p. 244.

11. David and Charles Livingstone, *Narrative of an Expedition to the Zambesi and Its Tributaries* (New York: Harper & Brothers, 1866), pp. 140–141.

12. Ibid., pp. 377–378.

Chapter 3. Who Was Henry Stanley?

1. Dorothy Stanley, ed., *The Autobiography of Sir Henry Morton Stanley* (Boston: Houghton Mifflin, 1909), p. 12.

2. Ibid., p. 62.

3. Ibid., p. 88.

4. John Bierman, *Dark Safari: The Life Behind the Legend of Henry Morton Stanley* (New York: Knopf, 1990), p. 28.

5. Stanley, p. 190.

6. Ibid., p. 200.

7. Ibid., p. 242.

Chapter 4. Stanley and Livingstone

1. Tim Jeal, *Livingstone* (New York: G. P. Putnam's, 1973), p. 287.

2. Dr. James I. Macnair, ed., *Livingstone's Travels* (New York: Macmillan, 1954), p. 291.

3. Ibid., pp. 362–363.

4. Norman R. Bennett, ed., *Stanley's Dispatches to the New York Herald, 1871–1872, 1874–1877* (Boston: Boston University Press, 1970), p. 96.

5. Ibid., pp. 94, 97, 98, 101.

6. John Bierman, *Dark Safari: The Life Behind the Legend of Henry Morton Stanley* (New York: Knopf, 1990), p. 117.

7. Henry M. Stanley, *How I Found Livingstone* (New York: Scribner's, 1889), p. 497.

8. Ibid., p. 624.

9. Macnair, p. 397.

10. Bierman, p. 127.

Chapter 5. Stanley's Explorations

1. Dorothy Stanley, ed., *The Autobiography of Sir Henry Morton Stanley* (Boston: Houghton Mifflin, 1909), p. 297.

2. Richard Stanley and Alan Neame, eds., *The Exploration Diaries of H. M. Stanley* (New York: The Vanguard Press, 1961), p. 32.

3. Ibid., p. 39.

4. Norman R. Bennett, ed., *Stanley's Dispatches to the New York Herald, 1871–1872, 1874–1877* (Boston: Boston University Press, 1970), p. 207.

5. Stanley and Neame, p. 72.

6. John Bierman, *Dark Safari: The Life Behind the Legend of Henry Morton Stanley* (New York: Knopf, 1990), pp. 183–184.

7. Bennett, pp. 380–381.

8. Ibid., p. 381.

9. Ibid., p. 384.

10. Ibid., p. 355.

11. Henry M. Stanley, *Through the Dark Continent* (New York: Dover Publications, Inc., 1998), vol. 1, p. 137.

12. Stanley and Neame, p. 203.

13. Ibid., p. 200.

14. Bennett, p. 371.

Chapter 6. Leopold II and the Congo Free State

1. Adam Hochschild, *King Leopold's Ghost* (Boston: Houghton Mifflin, 1998), p. 34.

2. Paul Halsall, "John Hobson: Imperialism," *Modern History Sourcebook*, August 1997, <http://www.fordham.edu/halsall/mod/1902hobson.html> (October 4, 1999).

3. John Bierman, *Dark Safari: The Life Behind the Legend of Henry Morton Stanley* (New York: Knopf, 1990), p. 226.

4. Hochschild, p. 68.

5. Albert Maurice, *H. M. Stanley: Unpublished Letters* (London: W. & R. Chambers, 1955), p. 49.

6. Ibid., p. 52.

7. Ibid., p. 47.

8. Dorothy Stanley, ed., *The Autobiography of Sir Henry Morton Stanley* (Boston: Houghton Mifflin, 1909), pp. 340–341.

9. Maurice, p. 160.

10. Hochschild, p. 72.

11. Joseph Conrad, "Heart of Darkness," *Modern History Sourcebook*, December 18, 1998, <http://www.wsu.edu:8080/~wldciv/world_civ_reader/world_civ_reader_2/conrad.html> (October 4, 1999).

12. Hochschild, p. 160.

Chapter 7. The Scramble for Africa

1. Thomas Pakenham, *The Scramble for Africa: White Man's Conquest of the Dark Continent from 1876 to 1912* (New York: Random House, 1991), p. 162.

2. Henry M. Stanley, *In Darkest Africa* (New York: Scribner's, 1890), vol. 1, p. 182.

3. Ibid., p. 142.

4. Ibid., p. 159.

5. John Bierman, *Dark Safari: The Life Behind the Legend of Henry Morton Stanley* (New York: Knopf, 1990), p. 278.

6. Stanley, vol. 1, p. 191.

7. Ibid., vol. 2, p. 412.

Chapter 8. The Legacy of Stanley and Livingstone

1. Paul Halsall, "All-African People's Conference, Resolution on Imperialism and Colonialism, Accra, December 5–13, 1958," *Modern History Sourcebook*, July 1998, <http://www.fordham.edu/halsall/mod/1958-aapc-res1.html> (October 4, 1999).

Further Reading

Books

Arnold, Richard. *The True Story of David Livingstone, Explorer*. Chicago: Children's Press, 1964.

Bierman, John. *Dark Safari: The Life Behind the Legend of Henry Morton Stanley*. New York: Knopf, 1990.

Cohen, Daniel. *Henry Stanley and the Quest for the Source of the Nile*. New York: M. Evans, 1985.

Farwell, Bryan. *The Man Who Presumed*. New York: Norton, 1989.

Hochschild, Adam. *King Leopold's Ghost*. Boston: Houghton Mifflin, 1998.

Jeal, Tim. *Livingstone*. New York: G. P. Putnam's, 1973.

Nicholls, C. S. *David Livingstone*. Great Britain: Sutton Publishing Limited, 1998.

Pakenham, Thomas. *The Scramble for Africa: White Man's Conquest of the Dark Continent from 1876 to 1912*. New York: Random House, 1991.

Internet Addresses

The Atlantic Monthly Corporation. "Is he not in Congoland? Excerpts From the Writings of the Nineteenth-century Explorer Henry Morton Stanley." *Atlantic Unbound*. 1996. <http://www.theatlantic.com/issues/96sep/congo/stanley.htm> (October 22, 1999).

Halsall, Paul. "All-African People's Conference Resolution on Imperialism and Colonialism, Accra, December 5–13, 1958." *Modern History Sourcebook*. July 1998. <http://www.fordham.edu/halsall/mod/1958-aapc-res1.html> (October 4, 1999).

————."John Hobson: Imperialism." *Modern History Sourcebook*. August 1997. <http://www.fordham.edu/halsall/mod/1902hobson.html>.

————. "Sir Henry M. Stanley: How I Found Livingstone." *Modern History Sourcebook*. July 1998. <http://www.fordham.edu/halsall/mod/1871stanley.html>.

Project Gutenberg. "Missionary Travels in South Africa." *Project Gutenberg Etexts*. 1971–1999. <ftp://sunsite.unc.edu/pub/docs/books/gutenberg/etext97/mtrav10.txt>.

Index